ANECDOTES *of an* ARAB ANGLOPHILE

ANECDOTES *of an* ARAB ANGLOPHILE

Faisal J. Abbas

forewords
Chris Doyle & Othman Al-Omeir

NOMAD
PUBLISHING

Anecdotes of an Arab Anglophile
Faisal J. Abbas

Published by Nomad Publishing in 2024
Email: info@nomad-publishing.com
www.nomad-publishing.com

ISBN 978-1-917045-03-2

Creative Director: Simon Khalil
Cover Design: Luis Grañena
Copyeditor: Simon Petherick
Translators: Sarah Sfeir, Joelle Sleiman, Joy Geryes and Charbel Merhi
Social Media: Jad Bitar, Nazar Khan
Author's Assistant: Noelle Manalastas

CIP Data: A catalogue for this book is
available from the British Library.

Dedication

To those who paved the way, a big thank you.

To those who got in the way, an even bigger one!

*... And to anyone who's had to constantly live with a
redline under their name on Microsoft Word,
remember: this only means you were meant to
stand out!*

CONTENTS

A POWERFUL ANTIDOTE TO OUR XENOPHOBIA

As a long-term Anglo Arabophile, how can I not welcome and embrace anecdotes from an Arab Anglophile? The last decade has not always witnessed uplifting times in the Anglo world, so to hear that, despite everything that Britain had visited upon the Arab World over decades, my friend and *Arab News* editor, Faisal J. Abbas remains an Anglophile is uplifting. That he has a love for these shores is even more heartening given that he confesses to having had Anglophobic views before living here. Something changed his mind over the years.

Forests have been felled to facilitate the huge library of books in English about those mysterious people, the Arabs. One book even conceived of an 'Arab mind'. Others tap into the Orientalist traditions of the exotic other, the belly dancers and the harem. There is even an entire literary genre telling fables of white western English roses falling in love with desert sheikhs.

Yes, the Anglophone world has for ages tried to explain and fantasize about these people and their 'strange ways'. A sackful of stereotypes abounds from dirty Arabs, to rich Arabs and, of course, violent Arabs. Faisal himself as a Saudi suffers from the enduring stereotype that any Gulf Arab rivals Croesus on the wealth stakes.

Having devoted over three decades to pushing back against this racist mindset amongst us Brits, I have been just waiting, perhaps dreading, for an Arab author and thinker to shine the light back on us. We in Britain are so used to critiquing others, especially Arabs, that it is time for us here in Blighty to be under the microscope, to have our hubris and arrogance challenged. All too often, British public figures climb their pulpits and lecture peoples from other areas of the world, including the Middle East, about their moral failings, often possessing the barest minimum of knowledge or experience of the region.

Yet do any pause to think how aspects of British life and history appear to others? How about our imperial, colonial past? Or our huge weapons industry and tendency to invade and bomb other countries? Do we stop to think how others perceive the widespread drunkenness and loutishness on our streets, which all too frequently is exported to tourist hotspots and football stadiums? I was once challenged by a classroom of Emirati teenage schoolgirls as to why it was acceptable to have topless girls on page 3 of some of our newspapers. I had no easy answer. Do we in Britain have a betting culture, as Faisal points out? Well, the NHS would not have had to raise an extra £100 million fund to counter the gambling addiction featured in the media in 2023 if there had not been a major issue.

Faisal tackles all of this with his well-honed charm and gentle sense of humour. His anecdotes are laced with friendship and warmth as he gently exposes how others find visiting England and, in particular, London where he lived and worked. He also pushes back against certain widely held Arab views of the English. For example, he argues that we are not mean or cheap but like to avoid waste. Yes, Arabs bulk buy food. Brits do buy half cucumbers, an alien concept in the Middle East.

Can any Englishman counter Faisal's arguments that we have dreadful customer service? Every McDonald's UK customer owes him thanks for his campaign to ensure greater availability of tomato ketchup at the fast-food outlets.

As a result, it is a devastating portrayal of our foibles and curiosities, including our perennial obsession with the weather. It was news to me, though perhaps not a shock, to discover that there is a British Water Tower Appreciation Society. It took being married to a Syrian myself for 20 years to understand quite how ridiculous having separate taps is for non-Brits. As for the 'dirty Arab' nonsense, for centuries, way before us Brits started washing, the concept of washing with flowing water was integral to Arab societies. Even now, Arab friends wonder at the lingering British obsession with having a bath, a fair point given how filthy bath water gets.

This book is a treat. It furthers much needed cross-cultural understanding in a friendly non-judgemental fashion. It celebrates our differences whilst delighting in our idiosyncrasies. At a time when Britain is becoming all too self-absorbed, navel gazing, often even xenophobic, this is a powerful and welcome antidote.

Chris Doyle*

*Chris Doyle has been the Director of the London-based Council for Arab British Understanding (Caabu) and its lead spokesperson since 2002. As an acknowledged expert on many Middle East issues, he is a frequent commentator on TV and Radio and a columnist for various publications on the region including *Arab News*.

ALWAYS IN A LEAGUE OF HIS OWN

For some reason, London is unique in the sense that it never ceases to inspire those who visit it, whether for a short or permanent stay. It is a bottomless well and an infinite river of history, art and culture.

Given the many waves of people who have inhabited it, its unique multiculturalism and the abundance of sights and monuments, one cannot help feeling that London is a place like no eye has ever seen, no ear has ever heard and no mind has ever imagined. This feeling is recurrent no matter how many times you visit, nor the years you spend living here. As such, it is not strange that a myriad of scholars, politicians, intellectuals, and asylum-seekers fleeing injustice, tyranny and physical and intellectual intimidation, have always written both about London, and from it.

In fact, one can argue that ever since the Renaissance, the British capital has been, and still is, the primary refuge for those who end up producing eternal works of literature that have influenced, and continue to influence, humanity throughout the ages.

Wasn't it in London that Voltaire wrote Letters Concerning the English Nation? Wasn't it here that Karl Marx penned the sacred Gospel of the Communists, Das Kapital or Capital? Aren't the London Notebooks of the great musician Joseph Haydn considered to be one of the best observations written about this city, despite their simplicity and ease of reading?

There have been many works written about the British and their capital. These works are very similar but unique at the same time. This is because we are human beings with different and changing perspectives; each and every person of the eight billion populating the globe has their own point of view. Fortunately, travel writing continues to help us understand them as it continues to occupy a leading position in human interests; it is a broad literary form, one which rebels against the rules that control other literary genres.

Still, capturing the pulse of a huge city such as London is not an easy task. Hundreds of tourist, scientific, and cultural centres as well as dozens of newspapers, magazines, radio stations and television channels try to do so. Alas, this is a city inhabited by millions of human beings, speaking 300 languages: documenting their lives would be a challenge for major encyclopedias, let alone a book.

However, my friend, Faisal J. Abbas, has successfully managed to do just that. Writing in his unique, sparkling style, without abandoning the seriousness of being a journalist, Faisal chronicles the ideas, impressions and impulses of an Arab living in the British capital. In its own way, this book is an ode to this incredible city. It is a reminder of its beauty and flair, and what it has to offer to renew people's passion for it. As someone who has been a Londoner for decades, and has travelled most of the world, I can safely say that I have never experienced the feeling of boredom that you get after spending a while in other cities; London has always been in a league of its own.

Perhaps that is why Faisal's experience has been unique and his anecdotes worth telling. As an Arab journalist, he too has always been in a league of his own. Hailing from Jeddah on the west coast of Saudi Arabia, he was not like many of his cohort who moved only geographically to the West. Many of them migrated, taking with them temperament, preconceptions and attitudes that were not in line with the new life they were experiencing. You find them rejecting the way of life here. They become increasingly attached to their heritage and customs, sensing that this will put them in a fort that will protect them from the winds of change and from whatever might scratch the crust within which they are contained.

Unfortunately, this results in two sorts of estrangement: one from their parents and land, and the other from a second life full of new ideas, experiences and things to learn.

Faisal did not follow that path. Throughout this book, he recounts a rich and deep experience. He gives us — his readers — anecdotes that straddle both cultures, and in doing so bridges a gap that can't be filled by those who practice fast tourism, just as fast food isn't as satisfying as fine dining.

As such, this is a book that elegantly dances between anthropology, history, satire and autobiography. The richly blended combination presents us with an exquisite work combining pleasure with enlightenment!

Othman Al-Omeir

Othman Al-Omeir is a veteran Saudi newspaper editor and publisher and has been a Londoner for over fifty years. His served as Editor-in-Chief of the London-based *Asharq Al-Awsat* and has been a prominent figure in the media for many years. His career has been an inspiration to many figures in the new generation of Saudi media professionals – the author of this book prides himself for being one of them.

CHAPTER I

CHARLIE AND THE CHOCOLATE FACTORY

I confess, I am an Arab Anglophile. What does that mean? Well, as one could imagine, it means different things to different people. For me, it means I burst out laughing at the humour of the likes of Michael McIntyre and would never get tired of watching re-runs of Faulty Towers and Yes, Minister. It also means that when I want to get my news from a serious source, I tune into the British Broadcasting Corporation (BBC) and read *The Times of London*. To quote Sting, I like my toast done on one side (and I may also add marmite, too). My favourite way to start my day is with a Full English Breakfast, and I enjoy scones with a cup of Earl Grey in the afternoon. New York or London? Are you kidding me? Beefeaters all the way! Besides, don't you find those Yanks at the other side of the pond just a tad too loud? Yes, I get that they are trying to be nice, but why do they have to shout constantly?

Yet, I must also confess: prior to being an Anglophile, I was a major Anglophobe. But it was not a phobia based on hate, as much as it was based on ignorance. Like many of my countrymen who were born in the '80s, we were mesmerised by Western civilizations. But for most of us, the West — which we dreamt of visiting and being a part of — usually meant the United States of America, or 'Amreeka' as we referred to it in Arabic.

Britain was more of a desirable destination for the generation of my late father Jalal and uncle Ziad (who went to Oxford). It never really emerged as a desirable destination for me and my friends, who were constantly 'California Dreaming' as the song goes. It wasn't really until the late '90s that 'Brand Britain' got a makeover thanks to the likes of the then young Prime Minister Tony Blair (before he got entangled in the 2003 Iraq war). The Spice Girls brought a new wave of music and the iconic Mini Cooper was reintroduced — 'Cool Britannia' was established.

Prior to that, I remember being bored as a young boy listening to my father's and uncle's stories. Their England was a quaint, old-fashioned land, forever sepia-toned in sentimental black-and-white.

Furthermore, the reality was that us Gulf Arabs are rarely forced to migrate. This is mainly due to the stability and economic prosperity in countries of the Gulf Cooperation Council: Saudi Arabia (where I am from), Kuwait, Qatar, Bahrain, Oman and the United Arab Emirates. Typically, it is the Arabs of the Levant and North Africa that have a long history and are still more likely to migrate in masses. Some asylum-seekers flee wars and drown trying to swim or sail to the safety of European shores, others leave for economic reasons and end up becoming very wealthy and successful in their new countries of citizenship, be it in Britain, North America, Latin America, Europe, Australia or elsewhere.

Yet, everything is always relative. Even within Gulf societies, there are many subtle, and sometimes unsubtle, differences. For instance, I come from a middle-class Saudi family, and while a day doesn't pass by where I thank the Lord for the blessings He bestowed on me, being surrounded by classmates who were driving sports cars at thirteen made me reach a some conclusions early on in life. As a young man, I was convinced that you could divide the human race into two types: the lucky ones — born with a silver spoon in their mouth — who always seem to get whatever they want without appearing to even try, and those who have to struggle and strive to achieve even some of their ambitions. I'd never won a lottery ticket and never passed an exam or got a job without really having to go the extra mile. Even romance seemed to require its fair share of diligence, and that was only made harder due to the now annulled segregation rules and extremist ideas that plagued Saudi society before the recent reforms which only began in 2016.[1]

The bottom line is I was blessed by realising from an early age which camp I sat in (well, the fact that the only sports car I owned at 13 was a toy that transforms into an action-figure robot made it pretty obvious). This is why I started working from an early age, and I worked hard.

The other blessing was an early passion for journalism. This started while I was still at school, and as I took on freelance jobs and worked on projects, I never thought that my work as a journalist would end up with me having to move to the West. This was something, perhaps unlike many of my countrymen and women, to which I aspired as an '80s child: I did not only want just to visit or buy products from the West; I wanted to live and work there.

Well, they do say, Be careful what you wish for, it might come true. I managed to make my way up the Middle Eastern journalism industry ladder early on in my working life and eventually, in September 2004 in my hometown of Jeddah, an envelope sat before me, unopened. For a brief moment, I almost thought it could have been that pristine candy bar that little Charlie holds in his hand in the

---

1 Since the introduction of Vision 2030, the government programme to increase diversification economically, socially and culturally in Saudi Arabia, all the previous guardianship rules relating to women in public spaces have been revoked. Men and women may now freely share public places and even hotel rooms without being related or married.

famous scene from Charlie and the Chocolate Factory.[2] If I opened the envelope, would I find my very own Golden Ticket? Tentatively, I cut the envelope open and there it was: a job offer inviting me to come and work in London as a journalist in the headquarters of most prestigious Saudi-owned Arabic language newspaper, *Asharq Al-Awsat*.

You see, just as every child who watched Charlie and the Chocolate Factory dreamt of winning a Golden Ticket, so I now felt like I had the key to a real chocolate factory: an amazing, desirable place filled with all kinds of unlimited pleasures. Yet this created a dilemma as noted earlier: the West for me as a child of the '80s had very little to do with England. It was more the technicolour dreamland of the United States of America that I aspired to go to. Why? Because, unlike Britain at that time, the US had an almost irresistible allure, fortified with its very own army of extraordinary cultural ambassadors: global pop stars like the late Michael Jackson and Madonna, Hollywood films like Rambo and Rocky starring the extraordinary-looking Sylvester Stallone, over-the-top celebrities like wrestling champ Hulk Hogan whose ring entrance song repeatedly reminded us that he was "the Real American" who always "fights for the right".

Everything about America was high octane, like a dial turned up to Number 10. Much to the dislike of my parents and teachers at school, my friends and I had pictures on our walls of the fabulous Pamela Anderson from Baywatch.[3] Our mothers and sisters were hooked on shows like Oprah Winfrey and Good Morning America to the extent one would think that their glamorous hosts and guests were talking about diet and dating problems in Jeddah, Buraidah or

---

2 *Charlie and the Chocolate Factory* is a masterpiece of children's English literature. It was published in 1964 by author Roald Dahl. It narrates the adventures of the boy Charlie inside the "Chocolate Factory" owned by the weird businessman Willy Wonka. The novel was adapted in two films, the first in 1971 and the second in 2005.

3 Although not so many people realise Pamela Anderson is actually a Canadian! There's an old English joke called Name Five Famous Canadians, and even as people struggle to get to three, they never realise Pamela Anderson could be added.

Abha...not NYC, Chicago or Houston. As teenagers, we wanted to eat hamburgers at McDonald's and ride cars like GMC or Caprice.[4] Like famous rappers, we were desperate to wear baggy jeans and slip into Nike shoes.

It's easy for today's generation to look back at starstruck little me with an amused smile. But remember, there was no internet then, the very first MTV video didn't hit the screens until 1981 (if you want to know, it was the American band Buggles singing Video Killed The Radio Star) — we didn't even have MTV, we watched those early videos on imported VHS tapes. Smartphones hadn't been imagined in those days. If you wanted to meet a friend, you used a clunky melamine telephone which sat on the table by the front door and hoped your friend was in to take the call. Going viral? Nothing went viral in the 1980s, there wasn't an electronic stream to spread the news in that way, so these larger-than-life Americans with their impossibly beautiful clothes and accessories...they represented the pinnacle of our desires and our hopes.

Britain never got a look-in as we fantasised about the ideal Western, i.e. American, way of life. Even when the English did produce a genuine star like George Michael, we assumed he must be American (to be fair, the fact that he wore jeans, cowboy boots and played an acoustic guitar when he performed Faith[5] might have seriously contributed towards the confusion).

The one thing the Americans did share with the Brits, however, was language.[6] My late father realised early on that the future would open itself up only for those who had mastered the English language, so he sent my brothers and I to Jeddah Private Schools, which were

---

4 One of the most famous Saudi TV commercials from the '90s for this car brand was: *How do you live without a Caprice?*

5 George Michael's single *Faith* was released in 1987 and the album of the same name went on to sell 25 million copies worldwide.

6 The famous English playwright George Bernard Shaw once wrote: '*England and America are two countries separated by a common language.*'

renowned at the time for their teaching of English from the first grade of primary school onwards, at a time when the Saudi curriculum in public schools didn't teach it until the seventh grade.[7] When we came home for the holidays, my father would set my friends and me English competitions in which we were required to search the Oxford English Dictionary, the Guinness Book of Records or translate texts from Arabic into English.

Apart from my late father, the one other person to whom I owe a debt of gratitude for my proficiency in the English language was Mr Egan, the man who taught me English in third grade. Mr Egan was a splendid fellow: a bald Irishman of advanced years, with rosy cheeks, he was full of vitality and positivity. He memorised the names of all his students and gave each of us a personal nickname.[8] If you got full marks in the spelling test, he would give you a postcard from Ireland or a postage stamp from another country — he encouraged us to collect stamps and got us to stand up in front of the class to talk about the country of the stamp in question.

At the end of each school week, Mr Egan would read and interpret famous British stories, dramatising them so it felt as though we were a part of the stories ourselves. Thanks to him, I read, at a young age, some of the masterpieces of British literature, such as the two novels of Robert Louis Stevenson: Dr Jekyll and Mr Hyde and Treasure Island.[9]

---

7 This has now changed, too — English is now taught in Saudi government schools at a much younger age.

8 Mine, for some reason, was Fazela!

9 Many of my generation only know these two novels as a Japanese cartoon series dubbed to Arabic and broadcast on Saudi television at the end of the 1980s. *Treasure Island* is a Japanese cartoon series (anime) whose original name is *Takarajima*. It was produced by Tokyo Movie Shinsha in 1978, based on Robert Louis Stevenson's novel of the same name published for the first time as a book in 1883. The Arabic dubbed version of the cartoon was recorded in Lebanon in the early 1980s, and actor Wahid Jalal was best known for his distinctive performance of the pirate Silver's voice. The series was very popular in Saudi Arabia and the Arab world, and some satellite channels are still broadcasting its episodes to this day; it is also available on YouTube.

Mr Egan was very popular amongst us boys and every day when he arrived at school, we used to insist on carrying his Samsonite handbag to his office, with him objecting and telling us there was no need. Others would take hold of his hand and ask him to play ball with us in the playground. More significantly, however, this teacher gave me my first lesson in geopolitics and history at a very young age.

Indeed, Mr Egan's popularity managed to provoke anger and jealousy on the part of some of the other teachers. In particular, I remember a maths teacher, who happened to be Palestinian, telling the Arabic teacher, a Syrian, that he intended to report Mr Egan to the school administration on charges that he was "enslaving students and making them carry his briefcase in a colonial way."

Nothing could have been further from the truth. We doted on Mr Egan and probably embarrassed him with our affection. But maybe there were other reasons to explain the maths teacher's animosity towards our favourite? Despite the fact that Mr Egan was Irish, hailing from Dublin, he was probably lumped into the "English" race in the eyes of many Arabs, somehow representing the sins of that country during its colonial years in our region and in many other countries around the world. No doubt Mr Egan would have been most affronted to have been labelled *Khawajat*, the pejorative Arabic term for the English people — as a proper Irishman, he would have bristled at the term.

As I grew older, I would regularly hear many Arabic-speaking men mutter furiously about the "double-crossing English" whenever some connection with Britain came up — this was the country which had occupied their lands, shared it out with France in the Sykes-Picot

Agreement[10] and then facilitated the establishment of the State of Israel after the Balfour Declaration.[11] We used to hear this kind of language regularly at home and from Arabic teachers in our schools, particularly since so many teachers came from countries which had suffered from colonialism such as Syria, Palestine and Egypt. Even our children's magazines regularly denigrated the behaviour of the British when it came to Palestine. The Palestine situation continues to be one of the most controversial issues in our society and will perhaps forever taint the feelings which an older generation of Arabs have towards both Britain and France. Many Arabs are proud of their studies, investments and properties in Britain, but others have not forgiven her for her actions during her colonial past.

The balance sheet for our beloved US, on the other hand, remained largely clean until the turn of the new millennium (until the 2003 Iraq invasion to be precise). The lack of American colonial activity

---

10 Sykes-Picot Agreement: A secret agreement was made in 1916 between the French diplomat François George Picot and the British diplomat Mark Sykes, with the Russians' approval. The agreement provided for the division of the near Middle East area after the end of the Ottoman Empire. Under the terms of the agreement, Britain took control of the areas between the Mediterranean Sea and the Jordan River in addition to Jordan and the south of Iraq. France controlled the south-east of Turkey, Northern Iraq, Syria and Lebanon. Russia was supposed to have Istanbul, the Turkish Straits and Armenia. The colonialists appeared to have absolute freedom to negotiate between them in order to draw the boundaries of these areas.

11 The Balfour Declaration, which is known in Arabic as The Promise of Balfour (although this constitutes a misinterpretation of the English term) is a letter from British Foreign Secretary Arthur James Balfour to the British Jewish leader Baron Walter Rothschild on November 2, 1917, for the purpose of transferring the area to the Zionist Union (an association founded in 1899 with the aim of creating a permanent homeland for Jews). The text of the letter explicitly stated that the British government was "looking positively" at "the creation of a Jewish homeland in Palestine and that the best efforts will be made to achieve this goal." But the letter also contains a part stating that "it must be clearly understood that nothing will be done to harm the civil and religious rights of the non-Jews there." Historians consider that the Balfour Declaration contradicts the 1915-1916 McMahon-Hussein Correspondence during World War I between Sharif Hussein Ben Ali and Sir Henry McMahon, the UK's High Commissioner in Egypt, who promised the Arabs control of the territories in accordance with the boundaries proposed by Sharif Hussein in exchange for the rebellion against Ottoman rule.

in our region over the previous century was obviously in marked contrast to Britain's record, and only its perceived diplomatic bias towards Israel in favour of the Palestinian cause sat on the debit side. Yet even this position was softened by the more recent efforts of US Presidents such as Bill Clinton[12] to reach a just and comprehensive peace agreement between the two parties.

America's popularity with many in the Gulf region increased when it supported the Afghan Mujahideen in ending the Soviet occupation of Afghanistan in the 1980s. This was followed by the US's swift support of her Gulf allies during Operation Desert Storm in 1991 after former Iraqi President Saddam Hussein invaded Kuwait. The Americans also intervened to protect Bosnia and Herzegovina's Muslims from the Serbs in the mid-1990s. I was so enamoured of the country that I proudly wore a T-shirt bearing the image of President George W. Bush Sr.[13] and the American flag, in appreciation of what the USA did to save Kuwait from occupation.[14] America was not just the land of my exotic dreams, it was also the great Western power which seemed to bring justice to our lands, not oppression.

So how did it come about, you may well ask, that I was destined

---

12 Bill Clinton was two-time President of the United States between 1993 and 2001. His relentless efforts almost succeeded in concluding a final peace agreement between the Palestinians and Israelis at Camp David in 2000. The Israeli Palestinian conflict has deteriorated ever since the collapse of his efforts at the turn of the century.

13 President of the United States from 1989 to 1993.

14 There is an irony in the fact that although the US intervention was invited by the wise Saudi leadership, which was credited with ending the occupation of Kuwait and cancelling the regional threat as soon as possible, and despite the popular welcome of U.S. forces by many, some extremists have portrayed the presence of these forces on Saudi soil as a "desecration" of the "land of the Two Holy Mosques." Internet forums and news television channels in neighbouring countries later contributed to this way of thinking in an endeavour to turn public opinion against both America and Saudi Arabia . Their goal was to serve the agenda of Al-Qaeda and its terrorist leader Osama bin Laden, who disagreed with the Saudi leadership when it declined his offer of liberating Kuwait with the help of his followers. Today, the American flag, especially after George W. Bush Jr. invaded Iraq and Afghanistan after the September 11, 2001 attacks, has become a symbol of hatred burned by Arab demonstrators from the ocean to the Gulf.

to move to England rather than America?

As mentioned before, I had been attracted to the world of journalism from a young age. I completed my elementary schooling in Jeddah and then moved to a boarding school of Rawdat Al-Maaref in Jordan, a branch of one of the oldest schools in Jeddah and Jerusalem which followed the British international system, IGSCE. In 1999, I began a five-year bachelor's degree at the Lebanese American University in Beirut, and it was during those university years in Beirut that I began to work as a journalist in the Future TV channel of Lebanon.

Future TV had launched the first Arab satellite TV channel targeting youth in association with the UAE-based Dubai Media City. The channel was called Zain (which was a play on words, as it means zen in English and "good" in Arabic). I worked hard at the job. I was a full-time employee of the station and a full-time student, with parents who expected me to complete my studies on time as they were paying my university fees. I worked at weekends and stayed up late at night to study when my journalism shift ended at 8 o'clock in the evening.

Future TV gave me invaluable experience in journalism, training me how to write and edit, take photographs and present TV shows. I was also paid well, with a monthly salary of US$600 which was considered a respectable salary in Lebanon at the time. But most importantly, I got to meet many Lebanese media professionals and Arab intellectuals. I began to write regularly, producing articles for the newspaper *Al-Hayat* which had just opened up new offices in Beirut's commercial centre, Solidere.

I graduated from university in 2003 and returned to Saudi Arabia to work with *Al-Hayat* in its office in Jeddah. But instead of feeling settled and content, I discovered I had itchy feet. The years of living alone in Beirut had liberated me; I had enjoyed the freedom afforded by a life without ties. Also, returning home as a young man, I was immediately aware of a change in the way I was perceived. In some cafés and restaurants I wouldn't be allowed in on my own — signs saying "For Families Only" would bar my entry.[15] If I complained about this to my family, the stock response I'd get was: "Well, when are you planning to get married, Faisal?" I had no plans and I resented the pressure to take this step. How was I to know when I would meet my future wife?

I began to think about moving abroad to further my career as a journalist. A former colleague who had worked with me at Future TV, Ephrem Al-Kossaifi, was now working with a US-government-funded TV channel called Al-Hurra. This was an attempt to win over the hearts and minds of Arab people who were angry over the invasion of Iraq. Ephrem offered to submit my CV to the Al-Hurra management and, once more, my dreams of America rose to the surface.

At this time, I was also frequenting a café called the Millennium at the Danube shopping centre on Tahlia Street in Jeddah. There were weekly sessions there where I could discuss and debate political and social topics with a close group of fellow journalists, academics and intellectuals. Sipping tea and coffee late into the night, this "Millennium gang" as I called us, used to evaluate each other's work and discuss different opportunities within media.

One of the most influential members of the gang for me was my late colleague Omar Al-Madhwahi, the Bureau Chief of the *Asharq Al-Awsat* newspaper in Jeddah. As mentioned earlier, this newspaper is one of the most important and established names in the Middle East; at one point it was considered the *International Herald Tribune* of the Arab World. Founded in London in 1979, it is owned by the Saudi Research and Media Group, the publisher of leading Arab titles including *Arab News* (where I currently work), *Sayidatti*, *Al-Eqtisadiah* and *Al-Jameela* magazine.

---

15 This was a outdated convention that was followed in Saudi Arabia at the time to give families and women privacy and space away from the supposed "harassment" of men. Security officers used to stand at the entrance to the mall, preventing young men who were not accompanied by a woman or family from entering. This practice has also been fully dismantled in the past few years.

Asharq Al-Awsat is still considered the most influential *Arab newspaper* (well, after *Arab News*, which I now edit — but you would expect me to say that!) As a child, I have memories of my late father reading *Asharq Al-Awsat* every morning. It would arrive at our house at dawn and he would read it for an hour each day, a cup of coffee by his side, always ending his daily ritual with the crossword puzzle. I was mostly interested in the weekly TV supplement which came out every Monday and contained stories about famous American TV stars.

Omar Al-Madhwahi was about fifteen years older than me and a truly great inspiration as a prolific writer. He was always supportive of any other journalist who produced good work, regardless of age or experience. As well as our professional bond, he and I shared a taste for good food — he could tear into a Porterhouse steak like no-one I've ever known since! We remained close friends and in constant contact until his untimely death in December 2015.

When we first met, I was both surprised and flattered to discover that Omar was familiar with all my writings in the *Beirut Al-Hayat* newspaper. He supported my application to join *Asharq Al-Awsat* in its Jeddah office and, once I had successfully joined, did me the great honour of proposing me for the newspaper's staff headquarters in London. Now I had a serious choice to make: wait to discover whether the American-owned Al-Hurra TV station would offer me a job or follow Omar's advice and join the London team of *Asharq Al-Awsat*.

My heart, of course, still beat to the rhythm of America, the multi-coloured, multi-cultural land of the free in my eyes. London, on the contrary, was still literally a grey area to me: all I could imagine was those black-and-white images of fog-ridden streets which my late uncle's reminiscences conjured up. Yet my Millennium gang friends urged me to choose London: Faisal, they'd say, a bird in the hand is better than ten on the tree.[16] Al-Hurra, they advised me, was a politically-sponsored American TV channel: what if the politics changed and the funding was withdrawn? *Asharq Al-Awsat*, on the other hand, was a highly prestigious newspaper and its London office had produced legends in the Arab media world such as former editor Othman Al-Omeir, who did me the honour of writing the foreword of the Arabic edition of this very book.

And so it was decided, with the arrival of the job offer and work permit wrapped like Charlie's Golden Ticket in an envelope, that London was to become my next destination. The doors of the West were thrown open to me and my flight was scheduled for the end of October 2004, which coincided with the holy month of Ramadan.

As the date of my departure came ever closer, however, I began to worry and, with every delicious Ramadan meal my beloved mother Alia prepared, I felt myself hesitating. Her wonderful home cooking certainly made anyone think twice. Each one would start with authentic Arabic coffee, various types of dates and delicious crispy samosa with minced meat or feta cheese, all accompanied by the Vimto Ramadan tradition. There's another British link which I had no idea about growing up: Vimto is hardly known in Britain today, and yet at least 20 million bottles of it are sold in Saudi Arabia every Ramadan. Invented in Britain over 100 years ago, this powered drink has now morphed into the most popular Ramadan sugary drink, requiring only water and ice to refresh the faithful after the day's fast.

In addition, my relationship with my late father was for the first time beginning to develop into a friendship. After my long years of study abroad, our interests had now become close: we'd watch action movies together, play backgammon, drink the Turkish coffee he used to like to make himself, and we'd talk for hours about history and politics. My sister and my sister-in-law had announced the joyful

---

16 I didn't know then that there was an English version of this Arabic proverb: "A Bird in the Hand is Worth Two in the Bush." Both mean that it is better for a person to be convinced of what he really has instead of wishing for what he does not have.

news that they were expecting babies, so I was to become an uncle. It began to seem tough on my parents, now that we were all united at home as a family, for me to announce my departure to the other side of the world.

At this time, there were also plenty of siren voices from friends and colleagues, warning me of the perils of my decision to move to London. One of my friends said that my decision was unfair, that I was in effect having a kick at the luxurious life I enjoyed in Saudi Arabia, especially since various companies and sectors at the time were looking to hire young Saudis like me who had studied abroad. They were offering attractive salaries; why would I want to turn them down?

Others whispered alarming stories to me. Strangers in London would try and slip drugs or alcohol into my food and drink. I would have my religion questioned, my values undermined by an immoral society. London was a filthy city, anywhere I found to live would be rat-infested. The high cost of living and the taxes would ruin me financially. As if all that wasn't enough, I would be lonely, because the English "were just as cold as their weather".[17]

I'm sure that many of these doom merchants were actually speaking out of their concern and love for me, but at the time, they felt like vampires who were sucking all the energy and ambition out of me. Today, I realise that most of them had never been abroad, had never touched their feet upon British soil, and didn't really know what they were talking about. As the famous poet Rumi once said: "When setting out on a journey, never seek advice from those who have never left home."[18] But without a doubt, these friends of mine temporarily destabilised me. It was my late father who came to my

---

17 It is known that the English weather is very unpredictable. You can go out in the morning in light clothes after you see that the sun is shining bright in the sky, to be surprised with heavy rain and dry winds by noon before the sun reappears shortly before the evening.

18 Rumi was a 13th century poet, scholar and Sufi mystic originally from the Khorasan region of Iran.

rescue. Fed up with my vacillation, one day he took a piece of paper and wrote down a career path for me, dividing it into five-year stages.

"You are going to be a journalist," he said. "Go now and do not return unless you are holding a Doctorate in journalism."

The final encouragement I needed came from one of the Millennium gang, fellow journalist Mohammed Al-Saaed, who laughed at me one night in the café.

"Faisal," he said, unable to control his laughter, "from the way you talk, anyone would think you were going to a famine-hit country, not travelling to London to work as a respectable journalist!"

The die was cast. On Friday 29th October 2004, I boarded a Saudi Arabian Airlines flight to London. After the air steward offered me Arabic coffee and dates, I closed my eyes and listened to the travel prayers that are broadcast on all Saudi airline planes just before take-off. I repeated the prayer in my heart, begging God to protect me both from the difficulties of travel and from having a change of heart.

And before I knew it, the plane was touching down at Heathrow airport. My heart began beating fast.

I had finally arrived at the gates of the chocolate factory!

CHAPTER II

GREAT EXPECTATIONS

For some reason, most likely my media background, the first things to which I am drawn in any country I visit are the billboards which stand at the airports or line the streets and public places. I believe these advertisements say a lot about the nature of a society, as they reveal a great deal about a country's interests, culture and even sense of humour (or lack of it).

Take Lebanon, for example. One can hardly ignore the advertisements upon landing in the country's capital city, Beirut. Not only are the billboards massive in size, but they almost always involve exaggerated images of stunning women promoting a particular plastic surgeon, beauty salon or celebrity make-up artist. This exaggerated trend no doubt upsets feminists and women's rights activists, but of course it's not really surprising when we learn that Lebanon — home to many of the Middle East's divas, artists and models — was considered the region's plastic surgery capital with a remarkable 1.5 million operations being carried out every year in a country of under 6 million people.[1]

On the other hand, when I visited Kuwait for the first time back in 2015, I couldn't help but notice that the airport billboards of voluptuous Lebanese ladies were replaced with juicy, giant-sized hamburgers promoting the latest "buy one, get one free" offer for Kuwaiti-owned fast-food franchises such as Burger King. Again, this isn't surprising when we learn that Kuwait now has hundreds of fast-food outlets and that the obesity rate of 40% ranks the country first worldwide in obesity, according to the World Health Organisation.[2]

Conversely, at Geneva or Zurich airports, which I visit annually on my way to and from the annual gathering of the World Economic Forum in Davos, it is hard not to notice the excess of ads for banking institutions and luxury Swiss watches promoted by international film and sports stars.

However, when I got to London in October 2004, it was the billboards promoting books that caught my attention. You'd find advertisements for the latest publications everywhere: in newspapers, magazines, airports and on the shelves of the railway station stores where travellers would buy books to read during their business trips or holidays. Of course, this was only four years before smartphones came on the scene and got us hooked to their screens for every spare moment we can afford. Back then, it was not unusual to see someone sitting alone, reading for hours in a café in London. You might also see a man pulling a book from his coat pocket and trying to skim through a few pages as he waited for his turn in the long line in front of the cash dispensing machine of a bank.

Even beggars tended to put their time to good use and attempted

---

1 Source: *The Media Line*, 2023: https://themedialine.org/top-stories/despite-econom-ic-crisis-lebanese-still-going-under-the-knife-for-cosmetic-surgery/#:~:text=In%20a%20 country%20with%20a,has%20gone%20under%20the%20knife.

2 Source: *The Kuwait Times*, 2023: https://kuwaittimes.com/kuwait-first-worldwide-in-obe-sity-second-in-diabetes/#:~:text=Kuwait%20has%20a%20staggering%2039.7,be%20 measured%20in%20several%20ways.

to educate themselves while they practiced begging in the British capital. Instead of the weeping and sobbing that we are often used to in many Arab capitals, a British beggar would find a comfortable street corner, pick up a paperback and dive into its pages while simply putting up a small sign for passers-by that said, "My dog is hungry, please help me feed him."

During my time in Britain, I also saw how publishing a book could turn into a nationwide event. For example, on the eve of Friday July 16th 2005, both young and old lined up all night at bookstores so that they could get the sixth book in the Harry Potter series. The book went on to sell nine million copies within the first 24 hours of its release, while the seventh and final part of this series sold 15 million copies — 11 million of which were sold in the United Kingdom and America — on the first day of its release in the summer of 2007.

It was only natural for me to start researching this phenomenon for an article that I wrote at the time comparing British to Arab reading habits. Sadly, if we take a look at the figures of Egypt's Supreme Council of Culture, an Arab reads on average less than a page per year,[3] while according to other studies a Brit used to — at least until recently — read an average of seven books per year.

As such, I was curious to visit British bookstores and ultimately became a frequent browser in Waterstones by Tottenham Court Road station and Daunt Books on Marylebone High Street. But curiosity, and my desire to learn, were not the only reason behind my new fondness for books. Reading was in fact my salvation from something from which I had started suffering severely as a newcomer: a merciless sense of loneliness.

Like most people, I spent my first days in London happily wandering around the city in the famous red double-decker bus, passionately taking pictures in popular areas such as Leicester Square, Knightsbridge and Covent Garden.

---

3 Source: "Study: Arabs Only Read a Quarter of a Page Annually", Qatari Al-Jazeera website, May 18, 2015: http://www.aljazeera.net/news/cultureandart/2015/5/18/

I also visited some of London's iconic landmarks, such as the wax museum known as Madame Tussauds, Hyde Park, Big Ben and Buckingham Palace. But the charm faded within a few weeks as the enthusiasm subsided, especially when I started noticing how my savings were quickly "vapourising" in this city, which was ranked at the time as the third most expensive place in the world.[4]

What didn't help was the arrival of winter. I still get a shiver down my spine when I remember how cold it was that year of 2004 and I am still unsure if it was genuinely freezing or if I had an exaggerated sense of the cold due to my emotional state at the time. Of course, heating systems, Scottish knitted sweaters, winter coats, gloves and scarves all helped keep me physically warm. However, I simply didn't know how to deal with how emotionally cold people were, and the "chill" that hits you when you find yourself in a big city all alone for the first time.

One of the things that troubled me was that neighbours rarely spoke to each other, and in most cases the conversation did not go further than saying "hello". I also did not take to the idea of someone putting their parents in a nursing home — this was very distant from our culture of extended family and caring for the elderly at home. Of course, I later realized that this was how many people cared for their loved ones in the UK, especially if they worked in another city or had no other option.

But in general, one could say that in the hustle and bustle of a big city like London, many things can fall unnoticed through the cracks and nobody is likely to care. This literally happened to my own mother who once stumbled and fell to the floor while shopping during a visit to London. It happened near the entrance of the

---

4 After the Cayman Islands and Switzerland, according to reports in the British News-paper *The Independent* (in the issue of July 28, 2015) based on Expatistan's study on the cost of life in different cities. http://www.independent.co.uk/news/uk/home-news/london-is-the-third-most-expensive-city-in-the-world-to-live-in-just-behind-billionaire-playgrounds-10422924.html

renowned Harrods store in Knightsbridge and unfortunately I was not with her that day. I was surprised to learn that no one rushed to help her or to check on her. She was left in pain on the ground for nearly 10 minutes before two Japanese tourists passed by and kindly helped her to stand up. Then they called a cab to take her to the hospital. Thankfully, the injury was superficial and by the time I got to her after excusing myself from work, she was fine and ready to leave.

I tried my best to defy the obvious distance and coldness and attempted to meet new people in public places, but all my attempts were doomed to failure. My efforts were often met with signs of wonder, astonishment and sometimes even displeasure. My frustration got to a point where I came to the conclusion that communicating with aliens might have been easier — and less complicated — than starting a conversation with an English person with whom you had no previous contact.

Of course, no one ever replied in an abrupt fashion. Still, the body language, facial expressions and brief answers of my fellow Londoners were enough to convey the nervousness that was running through their minds when I attempted to reach out.

There were also codes and cultural differences that I was not aware of, too. I recall an embarrassing encounter during the first months of my stay: the day I went to buy a new TV from one of the home appliances stores that fill Tottenham Court Road in central London. After choosing the device I wanted, the store employee brought it to me (she was a petite British veiled woman of Asian origins). It was in a huge box that she was obviously carrying with difficulty. Without hesitation, I rushed to take the load off her hands, saying:

"Please, allow me to help you with this."

To my surprise, instead of thanking me for my good manners, she answered coyly:

"Sir, please let me do my job, and do not assume that I am unable to do it just because I am a woman."

Such incidents were bitter and hard to digest. Although I was impulsive and desperate to communicate with people around me, these "social walls" that I was constantly bumping into turned me slightly into an introvert (unlike my true self), due to my concern about hurting myself or upsetting others.

Of course, when I spoke to my friends back home about these encounters, they were often shocked and said that this was certainly not their experience upon visiting London. But then again, tourists tend to have limited encounters with hotel or restaurant staff who are paid to be hospitable. Tourists also do not need to deepen their relationship with the place they are visiting or the people they meet, because they realize that they will be returning to their home in a few days.

This wasn't the case with me. I was here for work and didn't know when I was going back home. More importantly, I was determined to become a successful Arab journalist in London, so I needed to adapt...and quickly.

Once again, I turned to my books to further understand British society, to discover if what I was going through was normal. It turned out to be perfectly normal, according to the studies conducted by the Dutch social psychologist, Geert Hofstede.[5] He considered Britain to be the most individualistic country in Europe, where consumerism is widespread and where the path to happiness is through self-realization, not through collectiveness.

It became evident to me that this sense of individualism was more magnified in London, and even more so in Central London, where I had just rented a small studio – something which turned out to be a big mistake.

***

5 Gerard Hendrik Hofstede was a Dutch social psychologist, IBM employee and Professor Emeritus of Organizational Anthropology and International Management at Maastricht University in the Netherlands.

Like many new immigrants, for some reason I only felt safe in or near my workplace. I did not know my way around the city nor was I used to using public transport. Additionally, I was completely inexperienced. I did not know that I could have rented a much bigger flat for the same price I was paying for my studio (which I spent nearly a year in), with a separate bedroom, living room and bathroom, in a nice residential area that might have been just 30 or 40 minutes away from the office.

While my new home, or rather "shoebox", had the convenience of being five minutes away by foot from my workplace, it had many disadvantages. In the daytime, starting in the early hours of the morning, thousands of students, tourists and employees walked past my window, forcing me to wake up early even at the weekend. In the evening, theatregoers, diners and "party animals" made sure I never got a good night sleep.

Despite being a fun-loving person, I was very disturbed by living on New Oxford Street. It just seemed that the party never ended. You see, most people go home once the bar or club has closed. But this was definitely not the case where I lived. Many Londoners, after a night of heavy drinking, would continue to dance, sing and scream in the street till dawn. For some, their evening might even end at the hospital or the police station, after either getting into a fight or a health mishap due to alcohol-related intoxication.

At the risk of repeating a well-known stereotype, it would be fair to say that one cannot really ignore the excessive drinking habits of the British. This is despite the high literacy rates, public service announcements and repeated warnings from the National Health Service (NHS) of the dangers of drinking.

It should be noted that these awareness campaigns are only aimed at preserving personal health. There is no religious or moral obstruction denouncing drinking alcohol in Britain as, for many, it is a social habit that matches drinking tea or coffee in Arab societies. Of course, there are positive aspects to this "drinking problem": the British, in general, are very private and conservative during the day. However, as evening falls, and as soon as the glasses clink, they become completely different social creatures, and definitely more open and cheerful.

This is why one needs to be careful not to rush into thinking that you have necessarily made a friend with a person you have just met during an outing, just because you had a few drinks with them. It is not an exaggeration to say that there are some people who drink so much that they draw a complete blank the next morning, so do not feel offended if they have no memory of who you are and how much of a good laugh you had with them the night before.

Another typical winter nightlife scene is the unforgettable sight of scantily dressed young ladies waiting in line to enter nightclubs. In that bitter cold, where the temperature at night was around 5 or 6 degrees, I would not dare go out without wearing multiple layers, a scarf, a coat and gloves. You can only imagine my surprise upon seeing young English ladies wearing short skirts without leg warmers, coats or jackets! I know the sight of scantily-dressed, pretty women in any context is not something most men typically complain about. However, there I was, a full-grown man, shivering under layers of clothes while women my age or a few years younger were exposed to the freezing wind, walking around and socialising outdoors as if it was mid-summer.

Was it just that we Arabs were simply not used to cold weather? Have the English genetically evolved with time and ended up developing thick skin? I relentlessly tried to understand this phenomenon. Damien, who is one of my closest British friends, once simply told me, "Perhaps the weather was just not that cold that night." I then noticed that he too, was wearing an open cotton shirt, with no additional layers, while I was freezing my backside off during our conversation walking down Marylebone High Street. I should add that I have known Damien for twenty years now and to this day cannot recall him ever putting a coat on.

I later read about this very subject in a British newspaper: apparently, this so-called "mystery" intrigues the British themselves. While some think that the matter is no more than a teenage rebellious act, others believe that excessive alcohol consumption heats the body, removing the need for jacket or coat.

Another interesting theory was once published by the Daily Mail, in an article which spoke in particular about girls from the north of England, where the weather is much colder than London. According to this British newspaper's investigation, the phenomenon was linked to financial savings: many girls choose not to wear a coat to avoid paying fees for leaving it at the cloakroom. Who would have thought?

***

Being a bachelor, I spent — and still spend — a lot of my time eating out. In London, I tried to have regular spots to dine or have coffee in. However, this wasn't so easy near my flat on New Oxford Street where everything seemed to run automatically and emotionlessly.

There was a little Italian canteen nearby that I frequently visited to eat pasta and chat with the restaurant owners, joke with the young waitress and the old British Italian chef. The staff, who worked together for many years, seemed to me to be like a family. One day when I arrived I was surprised not to find the chef. When I asked about him, I was told that he had passed away that morning. I was stunned to see that the restaurant owners and waitress were all working, serving food and joking with customers as if nothing had happened. I would have expected the restaurant to shut down in mourning, but the owners simply said, "life goes on."

This was understandable, given that — and especially in Central London — local eateries needed to compete not just with each other, but with chains. I had developed a habit of having coffee at a French café near the office in Holborn, but within months it had shut down. It was simply unable to compete with global coffee shops such as

Starbucks, Costa and Nero, which were taking over the market and pushing their smaller, independent competitors into bankruptcy.

Since I mentioned Starbucks, it should be noted that during that same period (early 2000s), the global coffee shop chain had begun to spread widely across many Arab countries. In Saudi Arabia, the price of a Starbucks cup of coffee at the time ranged between £2.50 to £5.00, which was twice what we used to pay in local cafés (£0.60p to £1.60 maximum, around a dollar or two). In those days, to see someone carrying the famous Starbucks paper cup was a sign of their belonging to an international, upscale class, especially when pictures of Hollywood celebrities, such as reality television star and hotel heiress Paris Hilton, carrying those cups filled celebrity magazines. Suddenly, you found a lot of Saudi youth, especially those who studied abroad, insisting on holding their meetings, get-togethers or romantic dates in one of the branches of this café. For a period of time, you literally had to book a seat, as if it was a Michelin Star restaurant.

Of course, this was the case in Saudi Arabia but in London, as I came to discover, the perception of this American brand was very different. The impression I got among many of my British friends was that Starbucks was "way too commercial" for their liking. The coffee was "so bad" that, as one of my English friends later told me one day, you "had to hide its awful taste with a mixture of whipped cream, caramel, sugar and cocoa powder".

But it took a traumatic experience to make me realize how different the Starbucks experience in London was from Saudi Arabia. One weekend during my early months I decided to go and have my morning coffee and read at a nearby branch at the end of New Oxford Street. Because of the "high end" perception of Starbucks back home in Saudi Arabia, I had a shower, shaved my beard, wore my best jeans, a T-shirt and a sweater, styled my hair and sprayed myself with some perfume. Then I grabbed my coat, my umbrella and my digital music player, went out to the street and stopped on my way there to buy some newspapers and magazines to read while drinking my coffee. Arrived at Starbucks, I ordered a cup of coffee and a plain croissant. Because I was used to having my croissants hot in Saudi Arabia, I asked the barista to heat the one I had picked out, but he coldly answered: "Sorry, we do not heat up croissants."

I smiled and, intrigued, asked him: "Why not?"

He told me: "We just don't."

I told him that there was a toaster behind him, and a microwave oven as well.

The barista answered with a kind of fidgeting tone, suggesting that I was at fault just because I was not convinced by his "we just don't".

"Sir, please, there is a long line behind you, and as I told you we do not heat croissants, so do you want it or not?"

His response struck me like a lightning bolt, as such behaviour is unacceptable in our Arab culture, where it is almost forbidden for someone in hospitality to utter the word "no". I was genuinely upset, but I was having too much of a good day so I just assumed the barista was new or didn't know what he was talking about.

Obviously, the best way to enjoy a croissant is fresh out of the oven (preferably at a French boulangerie, not at Starbucks!). However, if you are going to reheat it, then just a few seconds will do, otherwise it will create a mess and shed lots of greasy flakes.

In any case, I went to a small table in the corner of the store, which was the only unoccupied one. After the first sip of coffee, I took my digital music player out of my pocket, plugged my headphones in and then took a newspaper out of my bag. But as soon as I was about to start reading, an obese, bald man bumped into my chair. Instead of apologising for the incident, he threw a worn-out tabloid on my table, hurriedly put his cup next to it — and in the process, accidentally spilled some coffee — pulled out the chair that was vacant and, just like that, sat next to me to read, without asking for permission or even offering to wipe the table.

Of course, I later realised that you simply cannot occupy a whole table for yourself and that it is actually considered inconsiderate to take up space with your bag or belongings, instead of leaving the space empty for others. Still, I believe to this day that a simple "excuse me" would have sufficed. After some thought, I decided to let it go, especially since the man looked messy. He was wearing a pair of dirty jeans that had stains of wall paint on them. More importantly, he was also neither wearing a belt nor underpants. Unfortunately, that last painful truth "unfolded" before my eyes, in every sense of the word: about ten minutes after his arrival, having slurped loudly through his coffee he got up from his chair. He then turned his back towards me, before bending over to pick up his phone, which had fallen on to the ground, and half of his rear popped up in my face, a view that ruined not just my morning but my appetite for the whole day.

Naturally, you do get world class service at the many Michelin Star restaurants across London, which I occasionally enjoyed during my time in the British capital. But I suppose the contrast here was that a clean, friendly and frictionless experience feels like a given back home, even at fast food chains. The same argument, I suppose, can be made when comparing the cleanliness of the Dubai Metro to the London Underground or the New York Subway. Of course, cynics would claim that we Arabs are just too spoiled, but this is not a fair argument, even though I can understand why people believe it. After all, Arabs did redefine luxury in recent years and did gift the world its first 7-star hotel: the Burj Al-Arab in Dubai. Similarly, many of my British or American friends would not believe that a McDonald's branch in the Lebanese capital, Beirut, offers valet parking services to its customers.

They also wouldn't believe that eating a meal at Kentucky Fried Chicken (KFC) in Egypt is — to this day — considered a luxury to many people. In fact, KFC is so highly regarded in Egypt that at one point, conspiracy theorists accused tens of thousands of pro-democracy protesters — who occupied Tahrir Square in Cairo in 2011, demanding and ultimately achieving the overthrow of former President Hosni Mubarak — of doing so because they were manipulated by foreign agents who had tempted them with free KFC meals!

In Gulf countries, most of the staff at fast food outlets either come from Asian countries renowned for their soft touch in hospitality, such as the Philippines, or they are professionally trained locals as is the case in many outlets in Saudi Arabia or Bahrain. You would rarely, if ever, encounter a problem with a staff member at McDonald's, KFC or Pizza Hut in these countries.

The same cannot be said for Britain. Here, these chains in many cases employ inexperienced teenagers or cheap labour from Eastern Europe (this was more of the case up until the 2016 Brexit vote which saw the UK leave the European Union). In many cases, employee salaries at these restaurants do not exceed the minimum wage, which was £6.70 per hour at the time I was living in London. Also, the British authorities frequently unearth employment violations, as some of these restaurants secretly hire minors or illegal immigrants, to save labour costs. It was not long before I realised that I had to lower my expectations when it came to customer service in Britain. But even so, I never expected to get bad service in the home of the Happy Meal!

One night, I finished work late, around 11.30 p.m., and was very hungry because I had skipped lunch that day. So I decided to go to the McDonald's branch facing Holborn station near my workplace. I ordered a large Big Mac meal and an additional cheeseburger. As I was leaving, I realized that the cashier had only given me one small pack of ketchup, so I stopped, smiled and said to him:

"May I have more ketchup, please?"

The employee's answer took me by surprise:

"Sorry, but we only give one ketchup per order."

I laughed, thinking that something was wrong, and jokingly told him:

"I have been eating at McDonald's since my childhood and have never heard of such a policy. Anyway, I would like an extra small pack, please."

However, the employee refused once again, so I asked him to call the branch manager. I expected the manager to solve the issue immediately, especially since the matter was — for me at least — very trivial.

But the manager (who was short, of African descent and had a bushy moustache) came up to me and said mockingly:

"Sir, I heard you asked to see me because you have a problem with our tomato sauce policy?"

I replied, saying that the norm is to put ketchup with the rest of the sauces (such as mayonnaise and mustard) along with salt, pepper and paper towels on a side table. I also added that if there truly was a "policy" about ketchup, the restaurant's management should hang a sign to let customers know about it.

The manager looked at me, and continued with his mocking tone:

"Do you really expect us to hang a sign about tomato sauce?"

I replied: "Why not? You have put up sillier signs, like those you hang near the restroom, which state that their use is strictly reserved for customers only."

Then, I added that I had not heard of this "ketchup policy" in any McDonald's branch I had visited in the world. The manager answered me coyly:

"Well, you have obviously never been to a UK McDonald's before."

Although I had had a very long and exhausting day, I tried not to show any sign of annoyance towards the manager's rudeness. Believing that I found the quickest and easiest solution, I reached into my coat pocket, pulled out my wallet and said:

"Well, if you don't want to offer extra ketchup for free, I am happy to pay for it. Let's just move on. How much will it be?"

The manager replied coldly: "Oh, sorry sir, we don't sell tomato sauce here."

At that moment — perhaps because of my extreme hunger — I

could not keep it together any longer and completely lost my temper. I fired back at him:

"Well, you neither want to give me ketchup for free, nor do you want to sell it! What kind of nonsense is this?"

I did not stop there.

"Have you ever learnt anything about customer service? The answer is clearly no."

The manager's eyes beamed for a moment, in celebration of his ability to provoke me. He answered coldly:

"Sir, if you do not like our service, you are free to leave."

He then turned around and went to the kitchen in the back without saying a single word. While my blood was still boiling, a young British lady who was standing behind me approached me and very casually said:

"Excuse me, mate, I don't like ketchup, I am really hungry and hungover and I have been waiting behind you for some time. If you let me order, I will just give you the ketchup that comes with my meal."

I felt really embarrassed and I apologized to the woman, telling her that the last thing I expected was for such a simple request to cause so much drama. I declined her offer, and left the restaurant after accepting the harsh reality that I would now have to eat my burgers not only without ketchup, but cold as well.

Not wanting to let the incident go, I contacted the customer service department at McDonald's UK days after that incident and filed a complaint against the manager. I explained to them my dissatis-faction with the scene that was caused, which I said could have easily been avoided. I told them that giving a customer an additional pack of ketchup was neither difficult nor costly, especially if the customer offered to pay for it. I also told them to consider comparing the cost of a pack of ketchup to the negativity that the scene had caused that night.

The customer service officer was very polite and expressed her deep regret for the incident, explaining that the matter would be investigated. She also thanked me for my feedback and said it was very constructive. I initially thought my complaint would fall on deaf ears, which is why I was surprised when I received an official letter of apology within a few weeks, signed by the company's vice president, in addition compensating me with a free meal coupon that could be used in any McDonald's branch in the United Kingdom.

While the value of the coupon was modest (£5, which only covered one meal), I think I came out triumphant, which is why I never used it. Somewhere inside one of my boxes of London belongings, it lies there with the letter I received.

Very few people know that I was the "unknown soldier" who caused a "revolution" for which ketchup lovers in the UK could be thankful. This is because, after that complaint (which was registered in early 2005), it seemed to me that the draconian "one ketchup per meal" policy had been abolished. No other McDonald's employee at any branch in the United Kingdom had since refused my request — or that of anyone I know — for more ketchup. Furthermore, you can now freely buy ketchup, along with other sauces such as BBQ and mustard at McDonald's branches across England, Wales and Northern Ireland.

Therefore, I can say that in less than six months from my date of arrival in London, I was able to change the system to the better. I didn't really expect to receive a "thank you" call from the Prime Minister or Her Majesty Queen Elizabeth as a result!

CHAPTER III

LES MISÉRABLES

As both a new immigrant with a limited social network outside of work, and as a young, determined journalist, I certainly spent a lot of time at the office during the first few years of my life in London. In fact, one could say that number 184 High Holborn, where *Asharq Al-Awsat* newspaper was headquartered until 2017, was indeed my second home.

Many of my colleagues at work were fantastic in helping me adapt. However, given that I was at least 25 to 30 years younger than most of them, my personal relationships at the office were naturally limited. Apart from a few exceptions, most of my new colleagues were married with children, approaching retirement and were living far outside of Central London. Despite this, I am happy to say that over the years working at the newspaper, I forged a few deeply sincere friendships with colleagues both younger and older. These friends remain very close to me and have remained so through thick and thin.

As for my relationships outside of work, I eventually resorted to mixing with London's "Arab Community". Again, looking back, I would also say that, although it took me a bit of time, I ended up meeting and befriending some truly amazing people. Some were born Londoners, others were immigrants who later became hugely successful in their respective fields and are now British citizens with a great contribution to society.

However, things were not easy at the beginning. First of all, as a new immigrant, you quickly realize that — contrary to the widely held perception — there actually isn't a single, united "Arab Community", but rather many divided "communities". For example, Iraqis in London are very different from Syrians, despite the fact that the majority of both nationalities would have migrated as asylum seekers, or in order to flee their home country's version of the Ba'ath Party.[1] Even among the Iraqis themselves, you will find that Iraqi Kurds have different interests, gatherings and hangouts than those of the Arab Iraqis.

Don't even get me started on the Lebanese, despite the country being the fifth smallest in the Arab World.[2] Lebanon has 18 different sects. During my time in London, and especially after the 2005 assassination of former Prime Minister Rafic Hariri, the Lebanese in London — like most of the country's diaspora — were rigidly divided between those who were for or against Hezbollah, the Iranian-backed militant group which eventually was accused of the assassination and later became the de facto ruler of the country.

Now, as a Saudi journalist, I would happily admit that I owe both my country and my profession quite a lot. However, during my first months in London, this dichotomy didn't prove too helpful, although I must confess it was very helpful in showing me how quickly people

---

1 The Ba'ath Party was a socialist political party founded in Syria by Mishel 'Aflaq, Ṣalāḥ al-Dīn al-Bīṭār, and associates of Zakī al-'Arsūzī, combining Arab nationalist, pan-Arab, Arab socialist and anti-imperialist interests. The Iraqi version of the Party ceased to function after the 2003 invasion of that country by the USA.

2 The four smaller countries are Comoros, Djibouti, Bahrain and Kuwait.

tend to assume and jump to conclusions. Since I always introduced myself as an Arab journalist who had recently immigrated to Britain, many were quick to think, wrongly, that I was a fugitive and that I was escaping intellectual persecution for political reasons.

Then there was the fact that I was a Saudi. This meant that many saw me as a "loaded", someone who could be easily exploited because — unfortunately — there is a false and outdated impression that as a person "coming from the Gulf", I must be rich – and naïve! Sure, there might have been a few tourists (and not necessarily rich ones as they tend to be more cautious and experienced), who were easily conned over the years. But in all honesty: name me one nationality in any tourist destination that has never complained about being taken advantage of? You hear the same stories of tourists or new immigrants being mugged, ripped off by taxi drivers or being sold things at exaggerated prices almost everywhere, and anywhere, in the world.

As for me, for all my faults, I wouldn't have ever characterised myself as naïve. And I was certainly not rich in comparison to my jet-setting, supercar-owning and party-going young Gulf comrades. Despite that, I still fell victim to fraud and scams, most of which happened, sadly, at the hands of my fellow Arab "brothers".

For example, I once dealt with a Palestinian lawyer, whose labour advice I needed. However, I quickly terminated my relationship with him after a horrible experience. I found out that this lawyer, who wore tailor-made suits, drove around in the latest Mercedes Benz and only met with his clients at the lobbies of the most expensive hotels in London, was able to scam many rich and even working-class Arabs by modelling himself as an Arab Harvey Specter,[3] albeit a much shorter, and one could say well-rounded version. He used to convince his victims to believe that he was immensely versed in

---

3 The glamorous lawyer portrayed in the American TV series *Suits* by Gabriel Macht. The series *Suits*, incidentally, was also famous for featuring the young actress Meghan Markle, who went on to marry Prince Harry and moved out of the UK.

British law by repeating a few legal phrases and taking photos with encyclopedia shelves behind him. He would always exaggerate the amounts he would promise to win for his clients and promise to humiliate their adversaries in court (which is something many of us Arabs find appealing, especially those that consider trials a place for personal humiliation instead of calculating their profits and losses).

This conman's practices certainly went against those of professional lawyers, who always make sure to prepare you for the worse. They then work to ensure the best possible outcome for their clients, while letting them know that nobody can guarantee what happens in court. That is why the wise thing is to always try and settle things without resorting to courts, something I later learned from a gentleman who came to my rescue, an English Citizens' Advice Bureau adviser-turned successful private lawyer by the name of Michael Newman (I am not giving you legal advice, but if you ever feel you have been mistreated at work, I would certainly give Michael a call).

Many of the incidents also happened due to my lack of experience. In fact, less than a year after I moved to London, I was conned by a Yemeni "brother" whom I had met through a friend. He took advantage of my restlessness at my New Oxford Street studio, which I referred to in the previous chapter.

To quote The Godfather film, he made me an offer I couldn't refuse: a house containing one bedroom, one living room, two bathrooms, a kitchen and a garden in the beautiful Maida Vale area for a monthly rent of £800 (£400 pounds less than what I was paying for a much smaller studio). Without hesitating, I got excited and made an additional payment of one-month's rent in advance as a guarantee. My mistake was to do so without signing a contract or acquiring a document to guarantee my rights. I just collected the apartment's keys and received a promise that the paperwork would be finalised later (amateur mistake, I know!) What happened after that was that every time I called my Yemeni "friend" requesting the contract, he got angry at me for constantly "annoying" him. He asked me why I was always worried. He always urged me to relax and reminded me that, as a resident in Britain, I had rights that did not allow anyone (he meant the authorities) to bother me.

Of course, I discovered that all his strongly worded assurances were worthless when I woke up, two weeks after moving into the property, to the sound of aggressive knocking on the door. At the door was a representative of the Council who told me that this property belonged to the State and was dedicated to low-income people (what the British refer to as a Council Flat). I was extremely confused, but I got away with it by explaining to him that the flat's owner had travelled abroad and that I was staying in it as a guest. The interaction ended with him asking me to leave his number and a message addressed to the property owner so he could contact him as soon as he came back from abroad.

It wasn't long before I packed my bags and moved to live temporarily with one of my *Asharq Al-Awsat* colleagues who had also only recently moved to London from Saudi Arabia. He had a spare room, and, since his family's arrival from Saudi Arabia had been delayed, he offered it to me. He lived in East Acton, which was not too far away from the King Fahad Academy.[4] Overall, I stayed in East Acton for a year and a half, then decided to move to my own flat in Fulham, where I stayed for the rest of my time in London.

As for my experience with that Yemeni conman who illegally rented me an apartment, it taught me not to rent any house, no matter how appealing the price is, except through one of the well-known and officially registered British real estate agencies such as Foxtons or Winkworth. There were also reputable Arab-owned agencies such as Lord's and Golden Eagle by Baker Street. Even though these agencies charged a commission, and negotiated hard on the price, at least you got to guarantee your peace of mind because their practices are

---

4 The school set up in Ealing in 1985 by the late King Fahad of Saudi Arabia provided Arabic language and Islamic education for children between the ages of three and eighteen. It closed at the end of the 2022/2023 academic year.

subject to the laws and regulations that preserve the rights of the owners and tenants alike.[5]

On the other hand, I don't know how I would feel about a particular estate office in Edgware Road (the famous "Arab Street" of London) that provides "3-in-1 services". The owner of the office advertises himself as a real estate agent, cellphone shop and provider of "legal consultation" services for issues related to immigration and residency. I don't know the link between the three activities or how a person can trust such an office – but you know what they say about "Jacks of all trades"!

Since I mentioned Edgware Road, I must say that it used to be one of my favourite destinations when I missed the sights and sounds of the Arab world — it was this area facing Hyde Park that would take me back home for a moment. The road is filled with shops selling all sorts of Middle Eastern products and you barely hear anyone speaking English (or it is very broken with a heavy accent). In addition to the Arabic newspaper and magazine stands which still existed at the time, there were barbershops and Arabic restaurants across the area. One of the most famous of these restaurants is Maroush, where you can indulge in a Lebanese feast of appetizers, Lebanese barbecue and Baklava. If you are in a hurry, you can have a Shawarma or Falafel sandwich from Ranoush Juice or Beirut Express. Maroush and all these Lebanese restaurants in central London, along with Randa and Sidi Maarouf, were owned at one time by the same person, Maarouf Abouzaki,[6] who in 2019 was awarded an Honorary Shield by the Lebanese Syndicate of Owners of Restaurants for being

---

5 I wrote an article in *Asharq Al-Awsat* on December 4, 2004, about my awful experience in this regard. It was titled "Renting a house in London: it requires a bit of luck and a lot of research and inspection skills." http://archive.aawsat.com/details.asp?article+269185&is-sueno+9503#.V50WiIN97Z4

6 The Maroush chain of restaurants is owned by the Lebanese businessman Maarouf Abouzaki, who immigrated to London to work as a chef and then opened his first restaurant with his wife Houda in Edgware Road in 1981. Today, the chain includes 16 restaurants along with a bakery and spice shop.

an Ambassador of Lebanese cuisine.

There is also Al-Amir (a.k.a Prince) Pharmacy at 99 Edgware Road. This pharmacy shot to fame and fortune, among the people of the Gulf in particular, for being the only one in London (and perhaps the world) that had the exclusive right to sell a "magical" formula called "the miraculous knee cream". Despite the cream's high price (a single tube of it used to be sold for £50), the demand for it was very high. Each time some of my friends, especially the elderly and heavier ones, used to hear that I was coming back from London to visit Saudi Arabia, they used to ask me to bring large quantities of the "miraculous" cream. According to the brochure of the product, which is based on a German formula, it can, in a single day, relieve the pain of people suffering from rheumatism, along with joint, back and disc pain – and sciatica as well.

Arab grocery stores are also found along Edgware Road, such as the Green Valley Supermarket, which was established more than forty years ago. There, you can find the imported products that you do not usually find at British supermarkets, such as Kashkaval cheese, Middle Eastern spices, Jordanian thyme, Palestinian olives, Saudi dates, halva, pomegranate molasses, and soft drinks that are loved in the Arab world but unknown in the UK, such as the orange-flavoured "Mirinda".[7]

Edgware Road also has a distinctive smell to it due to the numerous Shisha cafés found there. Wherever you stop on this street, you can smell apple-flavoured Shisha tobacco, with people smoking it from early in the morning until late at night. The cafés of Edgware Road came up with innovative ways to cope with the decision that

---

7 Mirinda is an orange-flavoured soft drink which was made for the first time in Spain in 1959. It was later bought by PepsiCo to compete against Fanta, the product of PepsiCo's traditional rival Coca Cola. Mirinda is very popular, especially in the Arab world. However, this product is not available in the British market, as there is another product called Tango, which is particularly popular in Britain, Ireland, Sweden, Norway and Hungary.

banned smoking in enclosed public places in 2007.[8] During winter, you can find the outdoor seating of restaurants and cafés equipped with heaters that allow café-goers to smoke Shisha in the midst of the cold. Some of these cafés still secretly allow people to smoke in hidden enclosed rooms that are usually located underground. These rooms are usually accessible to a select number of regular customers using a password in order to avoid municipal fines.

Although I enjoyed going to these cafés, it became clear to me that befriending the people that went there every night (including my Yemeni conman "friend" who rented me that dubious property) would only bring me headaches, as well as chesty coughs. Among those Shisha regulars were people who had been living in Britain for a long time but still, amazingly, did not speak English. This group of people usually had some problems due to the fact that they were not able to fit in their new society. Of course, some of them were also unemployed. Many of them relied on the assistance provided by the British government, in addition to some amounts that they used to get "under the table" (or cash in hand) for some services they provided or jobs they undertook such as deal-brokering, accompanying rich tourists and babysitting.

Among these was a Somali man who used to proudly tell us how he was able to trick the State and come to Britain as a refugee with his wife and children. Although the British government, at the time, provided refugees with a free home and a monthly salary as assistance, that scaled depending on the size of the family, it was clearly not enough for this gentleman. Apparently, he agreed with his wife that they would divorce each other "on paper" but not in reality. Given the fact that British law stipulated that single mothers should be provided with a house for them to live in with their children along

---

8 I wrote an article regarding this topic during my time at *Asharq Al-Awsat*. It was titled "Shisha cafes in London: are they taking their last breath?" published on June 23, 2007.

http://archive.aawsat.com/details.asp?article+424842&issueno=10434#.Vs4uCvl97Z4

with benefits and financial support, the divorced wife was given her own apartment. The husband and wife later secretly moved back in together and rented out the wife's new apartment "under the table" to secure additional income. After that, the wife submitted a new request to the Home Office in order to bring her brother from Somalia to live with her and get permanent residency and later British nationality. She claimed that, as a divorced woman, she was now at risk because she would find herself amongst non-Mahram[9] men. She therefore wrote in her request that she needed the presence of her brother to be alongside her as a Mahram. Of course, after her brother arrived in London, he might find a way to bring his wife or get an apartment from the State as well – and so on!

This was just one example of exploiting the system and this method was not exclusive to Somalis. I also had an Arab-British friend who rushed to marry a Russian lady who had apparently fallen madly in love with him, telling him she espoused "Arab family values". A few years later, having been naturalised as a British citizen as a spouse, and having had a baby with my friend, they got divorced. To ensure she pushed my friend to the tipping point, she made sure he found out she was having an affair with a Russian man. Of course, now she doesn't only have a British passport, but has her own home provided by the state because she is a single mother. Naturally, she may have her own version of the story. And in all cases, I believe any single mother must be supported in every way possible, regardless of the circumstances. It is just shameful, in my opinion, for anyone to deliberately try to hack the system or to claim for benefits when they don't need them.

However, back to the Edgware Road café gatherings. The shisha smoke was stoked by the fire of intense political discussions, which were mostly based on some highly imaginative conspiracy theories.

---

9 *Mahram* refers to a person with whom marriage is forbidden because of their close blood relationship. Many Muslims believe a woman may associate with a *Mahram* in her home without needing to wear a hijab.

A person once tried to convince me that a late Arab ruler had had a romantic affair with Queen Elizabeth II, which explained the privileges and huge deals that Britain landed during his rule. During another gathering, the discussion became very heated when it tackled the subject of the Iraq war.[10] One of the café-goers (who was a devout young man from Algeria) lifted his hands towards the sky and prayed out loud, calling for the destruction of Britain and the United States and "all those who conspire against Muslims."

I could not control myself. I stood up to leave the table when another person grabbed my hand and asked: "What's wrong? Why are you leaving?"

"Nothing, I simply do not want to talk about politics," I answered. (I actually feared a potential police or intelligence raid, but I did not share the source of my worry with the rest of the people there.)

The bearded young Algerian man who wished for the annihilation of Britain then arrogantly and loudly responded by saying:

"But my brother, we are in a free country. I am free to say whatever I want!"

I did not respond and simply left the café. However, if I could go back to that moment today, I would have said something like this:

"You truly are free, and this includes the freedom to be stupid. If God does answer your prayers and annihilates Britain on the spot, that would include you and your family too, you genius!"[11]

***

The only benefit I got out of knowing the Edgware Road secret

---

10 The second Iraq war, which started in 2003. The British government, led by former Prime Minister Tony Blair, played a pivotal role in it by advertising the idea and supporting the desire of the US President George Bush to wage it.

11 Needless to say, his prayer would have also harmed the nearly two million Britons who protested in February 2003 against the Iraq War. And also needless to say, the British intervention still taints the legacy of former Prime Minister Tony Blair, and his Labour Party, to this day.

Shisha society was to use them (without their knowledge) in a joke I used to tell my friends when they came to visit. I would ask my visitors if they wanted to go see Les Misérables.[12] They would agree immediately, thinking that I was talking about the famous West End play. However, instead of heading to the theatre, I used to take them to Edgware Road to contemplate those people sitting in the same Shisha cafés and listen to their negative discussions. I don't think they will ever change. Who knows? Perhaps the Misérables of London's "Arab Street" will one day become the main characters of a theatrical play – because after listening to their conversations for years, I can absolutely confirm that they do not lack the drama!

Yet, unlike these Misérables, I used to notice that English people and the majority of the other communities in London worked for longer hours but, contrary to what one might expect, they complained less! Most Londoners become overjoyed by the simplest of things. For example, the sun rising and giving the city a few hours of warm weather are enough for thousands of people, young and old, to go out to public parks and lay down on the green grass or go on a picnic with their friends and dogs.

The other thing I noticed that makes the British people happy and triggers their passion is their hobbies. The time they dedicate to practicing these hobbies is considered "sacred", and it is forbidden for anyone or anything to disrupt it. For example, I met a British public relations professional whose hobby was diving. She used to travel all the way to the Sultanate of Oman during her vacations and seized every chance she got to practice her hobby.

Perhaps the most significant thing I discovered about myself when I first moved to London was that I did not have any serious

---

12 *Les Misérables* is a musical play that has been performed in London since 1985. Running for more than 30 years, it is the musical play that has been performed for the longest period of time in the history of British theatre. The play is based on Victor Hugo's 1862 novel of the same name. It tells the story of social injustice that prevailed in France between the fall of Napoleon in 1815 and the failed revolution against King Louis Philippe in 1832.

hobbies. I soon acknowledged the importance of having hobbies for self-development and "mixing in". Through hobbies, you find people that encourage you to develop some specific skill, then some of those will become close friends. What probably characterizes British society more than anything is that there are unions and associations for almost all interests, from sports, poetry and stamp-collecting to bird- and butterfly-watching! Some might not even believe that there is a British Cloud Appreciation Society and a Biscuit Appreciation Society (that has three million members!) and a British Water Tower Appreciation Society.[13]

Since we are talking about the importance of hobbies and how they contribute to shaping one's personality, I must recount the story of a twenty-year-old English university student who loved surfing and lived in the coastal city of Brighton with four of his college mates in one house.

I visited him one night with a mutual friend. To my surprise, he knew how to cook Indian curry very well, which he made us that night. When I asked him how he was able to prepare that dish with the right amount of spices, he told me that he had learned it from his Indian girlfriend, whom he was currently dating. After the dinner, this young man (whose name I cannot now remember) made us tea that we drank outside in the garden. After he finished doing the dishes, he came outside carrying a long cane, the tips of which he wrapped with pieces of cloth, and told us that he wanted to perform for us. He lit the pieces of cloth and started performing dance moves similar to those performed by professional acrobats at the circus.

I asked him how and when he had learned to perform these moves

---

13 You can check a list of the weirdest British appreciation societies on the following *Daily Telegraph* link: http://www.telegraph.co.uk/news/newstopics/howaboutthat/11130610/Britains-weirdest-appreciation-societies.html?frame=2634439

and he told me: "Ah, yes, I learned it during the Gap Year[14] I spent in Eastern Asia with my friends!"

The dinner party was fun, but I was not able to sleep that night. It was not because of the hot curry spices, but because I was jealous of the skills and experience this young man had, which truly pushed me to think and compare. This guy had just turned twenty, yet he had travelled to Eastern Asia and lived there for a whole year just by relying on himself. He was also a good cook, he surfed, and his acrobatic skills were very impressive.

On the other hand, I had very few skills, and none that I would have liked to show off. Not only that, but I also found it hard to perfect even the less complex day-to-day matters. I remember how bothered I was by so many of these during my first days in London. I realise now that it was not a matter of me hating the city as it was about me being unhappy with my inability to cope with a new lifestyle that was based on total self-reliance.

When I remember the difficulties I faced, I think it would have been natural for me to think about going back to my "easy" life in the Arab world every time I burned a meal I was trying to cook, or was not able to read a road map, was late to something because I had been unable correctly to estimate the time of the trip,[15] or even paid

---

14 Gap Year is a tradition that a lot of students in Britain (along with other countries) opt for. It consists of the student choosing not to enroll in any university directly after graduating from high school. Instead, they spend this year attending specialised courses, training in a company, or travelling to live in another country and learn about its culture, customs and traditions. This is often done in exchange for very simple jobs such as serving at restaurants or cleaning yachts and so on.

15 Smartphones or Google Maps services were not practically available on phones until 2008, four years after I moved to Britain. That is why I used to rely on asking passersby and "my intelligence" to try to find addresses, which constantly made me arrive late. It was not until my friend, journalist Mohamad Chebaro (who was, at the time, the head of Al-Arabiya's London bureau) came to the rescue. After I was lost and had arrived several times late to our meetings, he gifted me the famous London addresses and maps guide known as the A-Z. After wrapping it with very fancy gift paper, he told me: "Dear Faisal, in this city, the A-Z is the only "holy" book that will lead you to the right path...so, do not leave your home without it if you want to live here!"

a fine for not reading the contract or the preconditions.

Even when I tried to outsmart the system, I failed miserably. For example, one day I was sick of the overcrowding at Covent Garden tube station. I found myself standing at the back of a huge crowd of people waiting for the elevator in order to get out of the station. So, I said to myself: "How lazy are these English people? Why don't they take the stairs instead of waiting this long?" Of course, I discovered after around twenty minutes, which is the time it took me to climb all 193 stairs that equate to 15 stories, why only I had stumbled on this "genius" idea! As you can imagine, I got to the top and exited the station short of breath, drenched in sweat and unable to feel my thighs because of the exhaustion. I felt so naïve when I later discovered that the station is filled with signs calling on passengers not to use the stairs unless there is an emergency!

I used to also make fun of the "cheapness" of the English people, but later discovered that it was not meanness, it was just being both economical and aiming to avoid waste — a huge difference. For example, I used to make fun of the availability of half-cucumbers in the vegetable sections of British supermarkets. This was because I was used to the traditional Gulf method when it comes to buying groceries: since most of us had extended families, it meant we were used to buying everything in bulk.

Of course, I later discovered that the British were doing the right thing. As a single person, I was not consuming a lot of the food available at home because I frequently used to go out to restaurants. This meant that the vegetables and fruits I used to buy in large quantities would mostly go bad and rot in the fridge — which is why, with time, I proudly converted to becoming a "half-cucumber" guy!

The other characteristic which caught my attention is how British individualism freed you from many unnecessary social and family pressures. For example, in 2009 a British Doctor named Steve Fabes took an open-ended, unpaid leave from work and decided to go on a trip around the world…on his bicycle! The negative consequences of this adventure were not limited to the fact that he had to leave his work as a doctor (which , in a country like Britain, made him a lot of money). It was also going to take six years, during which time he would visit 60 different countries under weather and political conditions that could be dangerous!

The reaction to such an adventure in traditional Arab society would range from accusing Fabes of being crazy to gambling with his career (and income!) having studied long years to achieve it. However, he only received support and encouragement from British society. Today, he is considered a star and a role model to many, especially after he announced that his trip would raise funds for a medical charity.[16]

On the other hand, there is no doubt that what bestowed the spirit of adventure upon many British people was the fact that higher education remained free for a long period of time. So, without the burden of tuition fees, individuals and their parents were able to afford the cost of various experiences and maybe even push back graduation for some time, allowing them to travel the world and acquire new skills. Britain continued fully to support higher education for its citizens until 1998, when the government of Tony Blair (which was a supposedly socialst Labour government!) decided to allow universities to charge British students tuition fees at a maximum level of £1,000 every year. These fees increased every year until they reached £9,000, as a result of a decision issued in 2011 by the coalition government which was led by the head of the Conservative Party at the time, David Cameron.[17]

What you also discover about "Great" Britain is that humility

---

16 You can learn about all the details of Dr. Steve Fabes' trip on his official website: https://stephenfabes.com/

17 The decision only included higher education. Basic education is still mandatory and available for free for students between 5 and 18 years of age in England. However, there are private schools (that charge tuition fees) for those who wish to enroll in them.

is among the most important qualities, while arrogance is socially unacceptable. English people do not tend to talk about themselves in general and will not welcome into their social circles any person who thinks of himself as the centre of the universe. Unfortunately, not a lot of Arabs realise this. For example, one of the deplorable Arab practices is the "invasion" of luxury cars — such as Lamborghinis, McLarens and Ferraris — that tourists bring from their countries every summer. The period between the months of June and September have become an annual event in London: these supercars can always be seen parked outside the most luxurious hotels in London, such as The Dorchester Hotel on Park Lane.[18]

Of course, the cars themselves are not the annoying factor, as many people take photos of them and admire them. It is rather the fact that many owners insist on driving these cars on the narrow roads of central London and in residential neighbourhoods filled with houses. Someone who works in the upscale region of Knightsbridge said: "I do not know why the owner of an expensive sports car, which is painted using a bright or metallic colour and has an Arabic license plate containing two or three numbers, feels the need to exert any extra effort to draw attention?"

However, when you ask some of the Arab tourists about this

---

18 The Dorchester Hotel is one of the most luxurious and well-known 5-star hotels in the world and is located in Park Lane, central London. The hotel opened in 1931 and was visited by a number of the most prominent celebrities such as Queen Elizabeth, before she got married, Elizabeth Taylor, Barbra Streisand, T. S. Eliot and Alfred Hitchcock, along with a large number of princes and prominent figures from around the world. Given the impeccable service which characterizes it, the hotel has a special place among rich Arabs who go there during summer and the holidays, where you find them sitting in the lobby for hours. It is also known that some of them drink alcohol in teacups so that nobody can identify what they are drinking or take a photo that would later be misused. The Dorchester also has a political history. The former Sultan of Oman, Said bin Taimur, stayed in the hotel from 1970 until his death in 1972, following the coup his son, the last ruler of Oman, Sultan Qaboos, led against him. On June 3, 1982, the Israeli Ambassador Shlomo Argov was also subjected to an assassination attempt as he left the hotel, which was directly followed by the 1982 war against Lebanon. The hotel has been owned by the Sultan of Brunei since 1985 through the investment authority affiliated with the Finance Ministry of his country.

criticism, some of them defend it aggressively, suggesting that it stems from the jealousy of others who are not able to have such expensive habits. Some even say things like: "They should thank their God because we bring our cars and spend our money here."

In the face of such behaviour, it was not surprising to see the obvious gloating in British tabloids when a picture of a Qatari Lamborghini being seized in front of Harrods circulated. The car was seized in late July, 2010, for illegal parking. This incident took place a short while after the Qatari state purchased the store. While the fine, estimated at £120, might not constitute a financial problem for the owner of the Lamborghini, which costs more than £1million, some of us need to understand that even if they buy all of London's stores, they will not be exempt from respecting the laws of the country they are living in!

Another popular location frequented by Arab visitors to London is Harrods. It provides a wonderful insight into the relation between money and authority in Britain and I must here mention the story of the former owner of this ancient store, the Egyptian businessman, Mohamed Al-Fayed. Who can believe that the British government, which awards its citizenship to almost 182,000 people every year[19] (including people with extremist ideologies, illiterate people, unemployed people who cost taxpayers money in terms of health services, education and financial assistance), rejected all of Al-Fayed's attempts to acquire a British passport, despite him being a billionaire who had lived in London since the seventies!

Of course, the issue is controversial because this Egyptian businessman was, for a long time, part of London's social fabric, a public influencer and on good terms with the most prominent

---

19 Source:

https://www.gov.uk/government/statistics/
immigration-system-statistics-year-ending-september-2023/how-many-people-con-
tinue-their-stay-in-the-uk-or-apply-to-stay-permanently#:~:text=There%20were%20
181%2C879%20grants%20of,the%20year%20ending%20September%202022.

international celebrities and politicians. He employed thousands of British nationals in his various businesses, which included — in addition to Harrods — iconic possessions such as the English football club, Fulham FC. Al-Fayed generated taxes worth millions of pounds for Her Majesty Revenues and Customs (HMRC). He also donated huge amounts of money to charities, such as the Great Ormond Street Hospital for Children. None of this granted him citizenship.

Even if a person meets all of the British citizenship requirements, the final decision is subject to the "estimation" of the Home Secretary, who can find that the applicant is not suitable to receive citizenship.[20] Despite the absence of clear answers regarding the reasons behind the rejection of Al-Fayed's application, some think that they have to do with a dispute, which dates back to the eighties, between the rich Egyptian and the late British businessman, Tiny Rowland, who was once his partner and later his rival.

The mutual accusations between the two included a complaint made to the police against Al-Fayed for using his authority to open a safe that belonged to Rowland in Harrods in order to gain access to confidential documents (an accusation the rich Egyptian businessman denied). Al-Fayed claimed the documents contained evidence proving that Rowland had paid the Conservative MP Michael Howard, who was one of the ministers of the Department of Trade and Industry (DTI)[21] back then, £1.5million in order to open an inquiry into Al-Fayed's acquisition of Harrods, which Rowland also wanted to purchase. So, when we discover that Michal Howard later became Home Secretary in John Major's Conservative government in 1994, the same year Al-Fayed applied for citizenship,

---

20 There is an elastic condition in the British Citizenship Law that requires the applicant to have a "good character".

21 According to the British governmental system, a politician could be a "minister" in a ministry without necessarily being the minister appointed to head that ministry. For example, there is a "minister" for the affairs of the Middle East at the Ministry of Foreign Affairs. However, he submits his reports to the Minister of Foreign Affairs that heads the Ministry.

one can begin to imagine why his application was rejected!

Al Fayed's second citizenship application, which he submitted in 1999, was rejected for no apparent reason by the Labour government of Tony Blair. This rejection came three years after the horrific car accident that took place in Paris on 31st August, 1997, killing Dodi Al-Fayed (the Egyptian businessman's eldest son) and his lover, Princess Diana. The late Princess was at the time in a romantic relationship with Dodi after having divorced the British heir apparent, Prince Charles. It is well known that Al-Fayed accused the British royal family, particularly Prince Philip (the late husband of Queen Elizabeth and father of Prince (now King) Charles III, and whom Al-Fayed used to describe as a racist and a Nazi), of setting up the death of his son and Princess Diana through a joint operation between the British and French intelligence agencies.

According to what Al-Fayed repeated on more than one occasion, the motives of this crime, which he was not able to prove, stemmed from the Royal Family's inability to accept that an Arab man was going to marry the divorcee of the country's heir apparent and that Princes William and Harry (the children of Prince Charles and Princess Diana) would become stepbrothers to Dodi. This narrative was officially disproved by the £3.7 million official investigation into the crash which was completed by former Commissioner of the Metropolitan Police Lord John Stevens in 2006, and which debunked most of the conspiracy theories surrounding the accident. The recent dramatisation of the events in the hit Netflix series, The Crown, also followed the line taken by Lord Stevens: the last series suggested that, contrary to widely held belief, Princess Diana hadn't agreed to marry Al-Fayed, and that the death was caused by an accident at the hands of a drunk driver speeding to escape the paparazzi.

It is worth noting here that, despite his controversial views, many British people stood by Al-Fayed. An opinion article published by the leftist Newspaper The Guardian[22] even called for Al-Fayed to be granted a passport, saying that he was virtually a "National Treasure for Britain" for his weirdness and sense of humour — like the time he tried to rap on TV, or when he asked to be mummified and displayed in Harrods after his death, or when he offered to finance the Scottish independence campaign in exchange for him becoming their first president afterwards!

Others thought that Al-Fayed was not aware of the extent of the damage his arrogance had caused British society, while some thought the Egyptian businessman's mistake was thinking that he could receive benefits and exemptions in exchange for the free "gifts" he used to give out.

As Henry Porter, London editor of Vanity Fair, which fought a long libel suit against Al-Fayed and settled out of court, said: "He just didn't understand that the British will take the money and disappear, saying 'See you at Ascot'."[23]

---

22 Source: *The Guardian*: https://www.theguardian.com/commentisfree/2008/feb/20/diana.monarchy

23 Source: The Economist – March 5, 1998: http://www.economist.com/node/115443

CHAPTER IV

ALICE IN WONDERLAND

By now, as you may have guessed, I had come to the painful realisation that Britain was not the 'pleasure island' I had imagined it to be when I first arrived in London. In fact, the only Chocolate Factory experience you will get on the British Isles, if you are seven to nine years old, is at Cadbury World in Birmingham.[1] If you're in the mood for a pleasant, informative and calorie-loaded family activity for your children, then this famous and highly popular establishment can provide just what you need.

In reality, the more time I spent in Britain, trying to understand its complex society, rich history and witty euphemisms, the more I began to feel less like Charlie from the Chocolate Factory and more

---

1 Cadbury World is a family visitor attraction in Birmingham which first opened in 1990. It provides a mix of education and entertainment based on the history of the old Bourneville Cadbury chocolate factory, attracting over half a million visitors a year.

like Alice in Wonderland.[2] Yes, that's right: if you move to London, once you are done feeling homesick and nostalgic, you have to be ready to dive deep down into the rabbit hole of trying to understand British behaviour, customs and metaphors.

For instance, why do us Arabs refer to London as Madinat al-Dhabbab (City of Fog)? Why is a British Public School called a Public School when, actually, it is a private school? Why do the British drive on the wrong side of the road, or is it the right side? Not to mention other sincere questions and embarrassingly inaccurate stereotypes that we Arabs, like many visitors and newcomers, hold about 'Great Britain' (spoiler alert: the name has nothing to do with British arrogance or the fact that their empire ruled most of the globe — more on that in just a bit).

But before I share with you the answers to all the above, allow me to start with some survival advice. The first thing you need to learn to get along with the peculiar, anthropomorphic creatures you meet, date and work with in London is the magical art of (are you ready for this?)...talking about the weather! You will be surprised just how many doors can be opened, obstacles overcome and embarrassment avoided if you simply join the national hobby of moaning about how hot, cold or wet it is.

Here's a classic example. I remember it taking me about five months to open a bank account when I first arrived in 2004. I won't bore you with the details but, to summarise, it was a chicken-and-egg

---

2 *Alice's Adventures in Wonderland* is a novel first published in 1856 by English mathematician Charles Lutwidge Dodgson (1832-1898), who used to write under the pseudonym "Lewis Carroll." The book tells the story of a girl named Alice who falls through a rabbit hole into a subterranean fantasy world populated by peculiar, anthropomorphic creatures such as a huge egg called Humpty Dumpty, the Queen of Hearts and the Mad Hatter. Since the start of the 20th century, this novel has been adapted into various theatrical, television and film dramas, including the famous 2010 film produced by Disney, directed by Tim Burton. However, *Alice in Wonderland* is known by most Arabs thanks to a Japanese anime produced by Nippon Animation in 1983 under the same title. The anime was subsequently dubbed into Arabic and aired on Saudi television and various other Arab channels during the 1980s and early 1990s.

tale where the bank wouldn't agree to open an account with just my passport as proof of ID, work permit and a salary certificate from my employer (which of course was registered in the UK as a British company). The bank insisted that I provide them with three months' worth of utility bills, but I couldn't get utility bills because I didn't have a residence or a home address to start with, and when I did, I rented a flat with all bills included (which was a convenient option, since I had no bank account to set up a direct debit for water, gas and electricity).

Of course, me being young, Arab and hot-blooded, I tried to go to different banks for months and argue, sometimes in a heated manner, with employees who were unanimously giving me the automatic, emotionally detached and frustrating response of "computer says no!"[3]

But I must say, I have to thank my lucky stars — or should I say clouds — for the divine intervention that helped me resolve this problem. One rainy day, I walked into a Lloyds TSB (as it was called at the time[4]) by Holborn station and decided on a different approach: I told the employee that I didn't actually have a bank account but that it was raining so heavily outside that coming into the bank and opening one was the only way to gain shelter. I capped this off by saying that British people all deserved a medal of honour for their courage in dealing with such miserable days.

The young Lloyds TSB banker smiled, shrugged his shoulders and asked me to take a seat. As he saw my green passport, he asked me:

"Oh, so you are from Saudi Arabia? The weather must be slightly different from what we have today!"

---

3 The catchphrase first used by the comedian David Walliams in the show *Little Britain* in 2004. He played the character of a bored office-worker looking up from the screen and uttering the infamous words to various disappointed customers.

4 Lloyds Bank merged with the Trustee Savings Bank in 1995 and traded under the combined name Lloyds TSB until 2008, when the group became obliged to divest itself of many of its TSB branches by 2013 after a European Commission ruling on state aid to banks.

"Just a bit," I responded sarcastically. But then rather than jumping straight into business, we spent a good five minutes back and forth talking about the weather.

The banker was fascinated to learn that we Arabs often refer to London as 'The City of Fog'. But of course, while the weather in the British capital is grey and miserable almost all year long, you rarely see fog anymore. Fog is these days by no means a dominant theme in the same way that justifies calling Paris, for example, the 'City of Lights'.

That exchange broke the ice and the banker was extremely helpful, explaining that they did have an offshore account option which I could open at once, which would solve my immediate problem. Once I had a credit score and enough utility bills, I could easily switch to a normal account, he explained.

Now, I don't know whether London is referred to as the City of Fog in other cultures, but I will share with you what I learned about the phrase. I hope this is useful, should you ever find yourself in a similar situation where you need to impress your otherwise extremely bored or not-so-helpful banker with some arcane knowledge.

From the 19th century until the mid-20th century, Londoners relied on coal for heating. As you will know, the use of coal results in thick smoke, which is released into the air through chimneys. When the smoke blends with natural fog, it results in the so-called 'Smog', which is very dense. Londoners continued to rely on coal until the 'Great Smog' disaster, which killed 4,000 people.[5] As a result of this disaster, the Government enacted laws prohibiting the use of fuels which produce black smoke in residential areas. Today, most British homes are heated with natural gas.

Now, this short historical background may or may not be that impressive to readers; what would be really impressive would

---

5 What happened in December 1952 was that smoke accumulated for five days, killing more than 4,000 people as a result of respiratory diseases, and even killing the cattle held at Smithfield meat market.

be attempting to explain the British obsession with the weather. The question is often raised in the works of many historians and anthropologists. After all, it is not like Britain is regularly exposed to extreme weather. In fact, British weather is known to be extremely predictable: it is mostly rainy, miserable and grey, and rarely sunny, hot and clear (with the possibility of snowfall once or twice a year). When we talk about London, we are definitely not talking about a city that is constantly being hit by storms, hurricanes or stifling heat waves, such as is the case in some US cities. And of course, the weather varies between "up north" and "down south".

Despite this, the British religiously follow the weather forecast bulletins on TV and the radio, with news about the weather regularly topping the front pages of national newspapers. As a journalist, I must say that every time I read a weather headline I can only applaud the creativity of my British colleagues who have to scratch their heads hard to come out with something different, unless of course there is a serious incident, such as the 2010 black volcanic ash clouds.[6] I cannot remember how many times I have read a newspaper headline in bold exclaiming that "this winter will be the coldest" or that "this summer will be the hottest"…followed by a familiar sentence written in a smaller font that reads "since records began."

Nevertheless, my survival and integration in the UK depended on my unravelling this weather-obsession mystery. And so I turned to renowned anthropologist Kate Fox, author of *Watching the English*.[7] She argues that one of the most important reasons why the British are fixated with talking about the weather is that it is a safe and general subject, and therefore, due to the British obsession with privacy, it is deemed an appropriate way to start a conversation with someone. (I

---

6 When the Eyjafjallajokull volcano in Iceland erupted in April 2010, sulphurous ash drifted down as far south as London. The UK Health Protection Agency said people might suffer from itchy or irritated eyes, a runny nose, sore throat or dry cough and anyone noticing a dusty haze in the air or the smell of rotten eggs should return indoors.

7 *Watching the English – The Hidden Rules of English Behaviour* was first published in 2004 by Hodder publishing house.

highly recommend *Watching the English*, which I first read in 2005. Not only did it inspire this book you are reading now, but it solved many riddles about my new society.

Besides privacy, the British are usually also unwilling to confront. So you need to understand that your intrusion, if I may, into their personal space puts them in an awkward position if they are unable or unwilling to talk to you. If you have doubts about the British unwillingness to confront, just try dining out with one of them. Whereas I — as previously demonstrated in earlier chapters — would make a fuss about not being served enough ketchup, a British person would eat a meal he or she didn't order, or not cooked the way they liked, just to avoid unnecessary drama.

In her book, Fox shows how to deal with her compatriots, explaining that it is better to start off by talking about general topics. My takeaway is this: if you want to talk to a young woman or man you like in a park, bar or café, avoid starting by introducing yourself, flirting with them, or inviting them out for a meal or a drink immediately. Remember, they don't know you!

The best way is to start with a neutral sentence, like:

"What a beautiful day, isn't it?"

If the young lady or gentleman replies, "Yes indeed! It is not bad; do you think it is going to go on like this?" then this probably means that they are willing to keep talking to you. However, if they answer you briefly and then turn away with a smile (or without), this means that they are probably not interested — get the hint!

Now let us suppose your quest was successful and that for argument's sake, you are a guy and the person of interest is a lady. You must remember to steer away, at the beginning, from personal questions. For example, instead of asking the lady: "Where do you live?" it is better that you ask: "Did you have to take the train for a long distance to get here?" By doing it that way, you would have spared her the embarrassment of telling you where she lives, if she doesn't want to at this stage. Or if she wants to share that information with you, she would say something like: "Oh, No, ...just a few minutes. I live in Paddington," or "Yes, it was a little bit far away, I came from Cambridge."

Of course, the problem for many expatriates is that it is rare that someone teaches you these rules, so you just have to learn from experience (or recommend buying this book to your friends, thank you very much!). There are also general rules of engagement, like choosing the right moment, to add to the above. Once I remember being evacuated from our office building in Holborn for a fire drill, and as we gathered at the assembly point, a dear, elderly and chubby Iraqi colleague tried to 'chat up' a young new blonde English admin assistant. As the fire alarm rang, and the public announcement kept repeating that we must evacuate the building at once, he held her arm on the way out and said: "Dear, what are you doing now? I want to invite you to go and eat."

Needless to say, my Iraqi colleague's attempt — as charming and generous as it was in Arabic — had the opposite effect on the young lady, who was slightly overwhelmed by his generosity to say the least. Watching this, I couldn't help but imagine Kate Fox covering her face with her palm and going "Tut, tut!"

***

Of course the British obsession with privacy is a mystery in itself. When I first moved to London, social media was not that popular or available (apart from a little-known website called MySpace) but it has been remarkable to see the British soak up social media as passionately as they do despite their privacy concern. Today there are 23 million Brits on X (previously known as Twitter) and a whopping 44 million on Facebook, sharing every imaginable detail of their lives.

Back in 2004, the big debate was about ID cards. Britain is one of the few places in the world[8] that doesn't issue government-produced ID cards (you can imagine my banking troubles would have easily been resolved if I had had an Identify Card that confirmed who I was). This is mainly because a large part of the population rejects the practice categorically and considers it a blatant attack on personal freedoms. While issuing such cards is a security necessity and is common to most people in the world, people opposing it believe in the right of the individual to conceal his or her identity if he/she so wishes."[9]

One might wonder what the aim of this stubbornness around identity cards is, given the existence of passports and driver's licenses (which naturally prove the identity of their owner). The truth is that I do not know the answer. However, a Briton who upholds his right to 'conceal his identity' will tell you that obtaining a passport or license is optional, unlike an ID card that — if applied — is mandatory.

It is also quite confusing to hear the British defending their right to hide their identity, when their country was one of the first to use closed-circuit cameras (CCTV) for surveillance and policing.[10] The UK currently has more than two million indoor and outdoor video cameras (an average of one camera per 32 people)[11] that monitor and record, moment by moment, everything that happens in a country of 67 million people. In many public places and shops, the face is not

---

8 Other countries not to use national ID cards include Andorra, Australia, the Bahamas, Canada, Denmark, India, Japan, Kiribati, the Marshall Islands, Nauru, New Zealand, Palau, Samoa, Turkmenistan, Tuvalu.

9 A good example is the organisation Big Brother Watch which said in 2018 that it stood up for "people's rights to be free from a database state and we believe information should only be held about citizens where there is a clear purpose or where they have consented. That is why we fight against the state's troves of 12.5 million facial recognition photos, 5 million voiceprints, 20 billion ANPR (automated number plate recognition) records – and much more."

10 The Metropolitan Police began to make use of CCTV in London in the 1960s to monitor events and rallies that were attended by any member of the Royal Family or Government.

11 Source: *The Guardian*, March 2nd, 2011: https://www.theguardian.com/uk/2011/mar/02/cctv-cameras-watching-surveillance

allowed to be concealed so that it can be filmed for security reasons (such as the prohibition of theft) or to confirm the legal age for selling someone cigarettes or alcohol. In this context, the subject of the veil (niqab) — worn for religious reasons by some Muslims — is the subject of much controversy in Britain between those demanding to ban it and those defending it.

The logical question here is: How does a person who objects to personal identity cards out of respect for their 'right' to conceal their identity accept, on the other hand, that surveillance cameras monitor most of their movements during the day? This is one of the contradictions I still don't understand!

Speaking of contradictions, there is a famous law in Britain called the Freedom of Information Act[12] that gives the people the 'right to access' information held by government agencies. But — believe it or not — there is at the same time another law called the Official Secrets Act that prevents workers in sensitive government areas such as intelligence officials from disclosing any classified information.

So: is Britain a country of transparency and the Freedom of Information Act, or is it a country of secrecy and the Official Secrets Act? I leave the answer to this question to Sir Humphrey Appleby, the famous fictional civil servant from the British sitcom Yes, Minister,[13] who is often referred to as the representative of tragedic bureaucratic comedy and its complexities in UK government institutions. In an episode which tackled the ambivalence of a government in a free country like Britain about withholding information, Sir Humphrey simply said:

---

12 The Freedom of Information Act came into force in Britain in January 2005. Originally mentioned in a Labour Party manifesto in 1974, it was again promoted in the 1997 Labour manifesto and then introduced as an Act of Parliament in 2000.

13 The famous British sitcom first aired between 1980 and 1984 on BBC2. A second series of the sitcom was produced under the title Yes, Prime Minister, which was released between 1985 and 1988. The sitcom reflects on the suffering of the newly appointed minister (and then prime minister) Jim Hacker in dealing with the government bureaucracy represented by the veteran Under Secretary Sir Humphrey Appleby. This British classic comedy has won several awards and has also had very passionate viewers. Among them was the late Prime Minister Margaret Thatcher who was so taken by the show that she wrote a sketch herself.

"It is only totalitarian governments that suppress facts. In this country, we simply take a democratic decision not to publish them."

And since we came to mention television programmes, I have to admit that, as much of a television addict as I was, it was really shocking to me to watch some of the programmes of modern British television which simply didn't make any sense and were nothing more than optical chewing gum that had no entertainment or educational value. Probably the last thing I could imagine is that a country of hooligans (famous for their enthusiasm for rioting and fighting in and around the football stadium) would at the same time watch a televised darts or billiards competition. Can you imagine how boring it must be to comment on such games? What can the poor commentator say except that the player hit the target with his dart... or that he missed! What is surprising is the high viewing ratings and disputes between television networks over the right to broadcast the championships of these otherwise not so television-friendly games. Of course, as we say in Arabic: "When the reason is known, the mystery is gone."

We must not forget an important factor in this context, which is Britain's betting culture. What one must realize about the British is that they are a bet-loving people. Betting shops — including popular shops listed on the stock market such as Ladbrokes and William Hill — are scattered on almost every High Street, and more recently available through websites and apps.

What do the British bet on? The answer is anything...and everything. You can place bets on obvious things like the result of a horse race, a tennis match or who will score the first goal in the final of a football championship. You can bet on which party will win the election, whether a monarch will abdicate or not or even if we will discover aliens living among us. One of the strangest betting stories was the refusal of Ladbrokes to accept a bet from a customer who wanted to predict the end of the universe. The reason for the refusal was, according to the company, the problem of the inability to pay the dues to the customer if his expectations turned out to be correct. A fair point, I would say![14]

However, the most important benefit I gained from watching sports on television was to understand the difference in meaning between the terms 'UK', 'Great Britain' and 'England'. Perhaps to some it might be obvious, but many do get it wrong. Some mistakenly believe that the name 'Great Britain' is given to the country for the purpose of boasting or bragging, as it is an empire that occupied large parts of the world. This is absolutely untrue, the word 'Great' in the context does not mean greatness. It means 'large' in terms of geographical context.[15]

The UK, as many know, is the acronym for 'The United Kingdom of Great Britain and Northern Ireland' (the full and official name of the country). Great Britain is the name given to the 'greater' (i.e. bigger) island states that include England and Wales compared to 'Little Britain' (the old name for Ireland, which is located on the smaller island).

Politically, the name Great Britain was first used after the Acts of Union were passed by the English and Scottish Parliaments in 1707, which led to the creation of a united kingdom to be called 'Great Britain' on 1st May of that year. Although, just to confuse things, the Scottish King James VI managed to become simultaneously King James I of England in 1603! The name Great Britain was chosen as a common term to refer to these two kingdoms, which were ruled by the same king. This is despite the existence of an independent parliament for each. It is further noted that the official title of King

---

14 Source: *Sunday Express*, January 25th, 2010: http://www.express.co.uk/expressyour-self/154077/Bizarre-betting-Top-5-weird-bets-you-can-place-today.

15 This term also applies to other regions of the world, for example when we say 'Greater New York', which means New York city and its surroundings: New Jersey, Connecticut and Pennsylvania.

James — the first and sixth at the same time — was 'the King of Great Brittaine, Ireland and France' (although he did not rule France!)[16] Ireland was entirely part of the United Kingdom until 1922, when most parts of that country became independent to form the Irish Republic. Northern Ireland has remained part of the UK to this day.

Speaking of betting, sports watching and the British, I bet you are now wondering what on earth I am getting to and what does this quick lesson in history and geography have to do with televised sports matches? Well, you have just decided to dive deeper into Alice's rabbit hole...

Although the UK is officially one country, it does not play under that name at the Olympics, for instance. The country is represented by a national team called Team GB which is supposed to mean only England, Scotland and Wales... but in this case, however, it also includes Northern Ireland.

Yet, during the World Cup and the UEFA European Championships, the UK participates as four independent teams, one team for England, another for Scotland, a third for Wales and a fourth for Northern Ireland. But just because it is like that in football, it doesn't mean it is the same in rugby, where the Republic of Ireland (which is independent of the United Kingdom) and Northern Ireland (a part of the United Kingdom) form one team and play together.

Don't worry! You are not the only one who thinks it is complicated. The British themselves cannot understand it either. Among the recent and related complications was the UK's announcement that the GB Football Team would not participate in the 2016 Rio de Janeiro Olympics. The reason was the Football Associations of Scotland, Wales and Northern Ireland rejected the English Football Association's

---

16 Since the time of Edward III, some of the kings of England have given themselves the right to ascend the throne in France by the fact that the mother of King Edward III is a French princess. According to the laws of the British throne at the time, this gave him the right to rule France, but the law itself was not applicable in France, which denied women the throne or to undertake the covenant through female lineage.

proposal to play as one team. Then former Welsh Association President Trefor Lloyd Hughes launched, before the Olympics, an unprecedented media attack on the English Association (the largest and richest of the four associations), accusing it of wanting to "take over everything."[17]

In this context, we must remember that we are talking about four countries that have a bloody history among themselves, and have fought over so many things besides football. Although there has been a union between them for hundreds of years, most of the inhabitants of the kingdom's different regions still identify themselves as English, Scots, Welsh or Northern Irish before saying they are British.

We should also remember that there is a huge chunk of the English population which would prefer to give up the monarchy and become a republic,[18] and that many Scots have sought and still are seeking independence for their country.[19] This is the same as many Northern Irish, of whom a separatist group, known as the Irish Republican Army (IRA), accused of terror for a long time, fought a fierce war to separate from the United Kingdom and unite with the Irish Republic.[20] When we take all that into consideration we then must wonder: is this kingdom actually united?

---

17 Source:

Sky Sports, 24th March 2015: https://www.skysports.com/football/news/12010/9773775/welsh-fa-president-hits-out-at-the-football-association

18 Several polls have been conducted on the subject, and although the majority voted for keeping the monarchy, this majority decreased to only 65 percent of the population in 2005, according to a poll by Murray on the sidelines of the then Prince Charles's marriage to his second wife Camilla Parker-Bowles. A further poll by Ipsos in 2022 showed that the majority had fallen once more to 60%: https://www.ipsos.com/en-uk/three-five-favour-britain-remaining-monarchy-although-support-falls-2012-peak-more-become-0

19 On September 8th, 2014, a referendum was held in Scotland regarding the independence from the United Kingdom. While the result was in favour of those who voted 'No' (55.3%), those who voted 'Yes' formed a significant percentage (44.7%).

20 The Belfast Agreement also known as the Good Friday Agreement signed on 10th April 1998 ended some 30 years of political problems and bloodshed. The agreement organized the relationship between the Irish Republic and Northern Ireland, between Northern Ireland and the United Kingdom and between the Irish Republic and the United Kingdom.

The other thing we need to know about the countries that form the UK is the difference in religious affiliations. Most English and Welsh follow the Anglican Church headed by a British monarch, the majority of Scots Christians follow the Protestant Presbyterian Church of the Kirk, while the Irish are divided between being a slight majority of Protestants in Northern Ireland, and Catholics making up a far bigger majority of the Republic of Ireland, which is independent of the UK as we mentioned before.

On the other hand, every country in the United Kingdom has its own language. Although this is not an obstacle as English is the official and first language of the kingdom, that does not mean that all the country's population speaks it in the same way. The English dialect is not only different from that of the Scots or the Irish, but also the dialects are varied according to different regions of England. The Northern English dialect (that of Newcastle residents for example) is quite different from the dialect of Southerners such as Londoners.

As for me, I faced a real problem when I came to the UK. Although I was aware that my culture was largely American, what I did not properly appreciate was the magnitude of the disparity between American and British cultures...and the extreme difference in the expressions and words used, which may mean two totally different things.

Perhaps the best example of this is the variation in vocabulary that is supposed to refer to the same thing in English. For example, the first term I could not understand — which I encountered looking for an apartment to live in — was the British use of the word 'flat'. In the Arab world, we use the term 'apartment' as Americans do, a derivation of the French 'appartement' and the Italian 'appartimento'. The British, however, took to the word 'flat' because that is literally what it was: there were no stairs.

In restaurants, we Arabs say 'fries' not 'chips' when we order French fries. On the other hand, for us, as is the case with Americans, 'lemonade' is lemon juice mixed with water and sugar, not a name for the soft drink that we know as '7Up' or 'Sprite'. After eating, we ask the waiter for the 'check' not the 'bill'.

Also, we usually say 'pants', while the British use the word 'trousers'. They use 'pants' to refer to men's underpants or 'boxers' as most of us call them. And yes, I wouldn't go down there unless I had a story related to a pants vs trousers mix up!

The story is that I did not realize that there was a difference between the British and American terms, until one night I asked my BBC friend Damien — innocently — if he liked my pants. (It was at a party at a mutual friend's house during my first January in London.) At the time, I was boasting that I had bought the pants at a big discount during the sale season that follows Christmas Day.[21] I used the term 'pants' saying: "Damian, do you like my new pants?" I did not then realise it would mean, in British terms, that I was asking my friend what he thought of my underpants! Damian answered me sarcastically: "Well, I can't really see them, Faisal!"

Of course, I blushed when Damien explained the difference to me. The next day, I bought a dictionary of British terms and corresponding American words. However, this was not enough to solve all my problems with the language, as when it came to understanding the English's English, you really need to either be English or just accept that things may simply not make any sense at all. And why not? This is a tolerant nation after all.

For example, when you say 'public school' anywhere in the world, it probably means a government-funded school, or state-funded school for the public. But the situation is different in Britain, where the term holds the exact opposite meaning. It means a private school that is not managed or funded by the government (in return, the state/free school in Britain is called 'state school'). British public

---

21 Most stores in Britain announce major discounts the day after Christmas Day, December 26th each year, known as Boxing Day. There are several theories about the origin of the label, but the most common is the tradition of masters or employers giving their servants and helpers gift "boxes" the day after Christmas.

schools are not only private, but largely elitist. Their annual tuition fees amount to about £35,000.[22] These schools also compete among themselves — to graduate the country's future leaders. Seven British prime ministers, including Winston Churchill, graduated from Harrow School (founded in 1572). There is also Eton school, founded in 1440, from which 20 British prime ministers graduated, most recently Boris Johnson, who served as Prime Minister between 2019 and 2022.

Another thing that 'public schools' are known for is the unique accent that distinguishes those who study in them. The accent clearly emphasises the deliberate and perhaps languorous articulation of every letter vowel, as opposed to, say, a Cockney accent, the East London working class accent, which is characterised by omitting some letters or combining them together.

My own accent — which was largely influenced by years and years of watching MTV and Hollywood movies — had a negative impact on me in Britain, which I didn't at first realise. There is an important cultural difference here, because speaking with an American accent may be favourable in the Arab world, as it gives the impression that you are a modern, globalised guy who got a good education abroad.[23] However, I soon realised that sounding like a Yank didn't do me any favours in Britain. According to some of my friends who now remember my early days in London, my heavy American accent made me sound both snobbish and 'ungenuine'.

The British often criticise Americans' loud speaking voices and the heightened sense of self-confidence when they speak. Being cynical by nature, the British mostly believe that Americans are drama queens, that they brag way too much about their 'achievements' and

---

22 Source: St James's Place: https://www.sjp.co.uk/news/how-much-does-private-education-cost

23 As opposed to those who speak English in a heavy Arabic dialect. Examples of this dialect includes confusing the letter P and the letter B, pronouncing two words together (such as saying 'Oxforestreet' instead of Oxford Street) or pronouncing the silent letters, like the letter 'K' in the word 'Knightsbridge'.

that they have a false belief that they are better than everyone else.

For example, I still remember the dark humour and comments that an old, witty and very English university professor voiced on the night that followed President Barack Obama's election. As the whole world celebrated Obama's victory as the first black president of the United States in 2008, this elderly Englishman grumbled about the over-attention given to this subject, dominating the headlines in all media outlets. He said sarcastically — and coldly — while drinking beer in a bar full of American students who were cheering and wearing their stars and stripes: "What's this fuss all about, it is not like the Yanks elected a Native American as President!"[24]

The contrast between British and Americans is not just limited to dialect and different vocabulary meanings. It extends to units of measurement that may have the same name but vary in capacity (e.g. U.S. gallon capacity is lower than British imperial gallon capacity). And you can't buy British eggs in American stores and vice versa – American eggs are not allowed to be sold in British stores.[25] There is also the issue of driving on the left in the UK, as well as 76 other countries around the world, mostly former British colonies such as India, Australia and Hong Kong.[26] Another distinctive British phenomenon is that you find separate taps for hot and cold water in traditional washrooms — apparently these were introduced in the

---

24 The election of the first black President of the United States was a massive landmark in American and world history. I suspect my old English university professor might think twice about making such a provocative comment in today's world.

25 The U.S. Department of Agriculture prohibits selling British eggs, because it requires washing eggs with water and spraying them with a chemical disinfectant before selling them in stores, which is actually carried out in the U.S. Britain, by contrast forbids American eggs because they prevent eggs from being washed and sprayed before they are sold, on the basis that the cleaning agents might be toxic.

26 According to historians, driving was originally on the left since the time of the Roman carts. Because most people use their right arm, it was a good idea for a person to ride their horse on the left side, leaving more room for taking the sword out of the sheath (usually on a person's left flank) in the event of being attacked by someone, particularly important in medieval jousting contests.

19th century because the cold water supply was deemed purer than hot water which had been stored in a tank in the attic. This, again, is surprising for many visitors.

Then there is the big difference in the laws and regulations between the United States and Britain. It is well known that Americans are entitled according to the constitution to own and use guns and weapons for self-defence. This is not only illegal in the UK, but it is regarded as a barbaric. The use of knives in crime in London upsets British people, but a school shooting (or a series of them) such as in America is simply unthinkable in Britain.

Here's another example: the difference in dealing with someone trespassing onto your home or land that you own. In the United States, it is against the law to squat in a property owned by another person. More liberal Americans would immediately contact the police to force the intruder to leave, while those who religiously believe in the second amendment would immediately resort to taking their rights into their own hands, literally. In a state like Texas, it wouldn't be unusual to read signs outside homes that say: "Trespassers will be shot."

Meanwhile would you believe that squatting in residential homes was not against the law in Britain until a change in legislation in 2012? In other words, until recently, you couldn't do anything to evict a group of squatters if they gained access to your home without breaking in while you were away and they decided to stay there. The story doesn't end there: would you believe that there is a British association that actually protects squatters and gives them advice? This of course doesn't exist to help property owners, but is in aid and support for squatters, since many of them are usually homeless and have no shelter to live in. The association is known as the Advisory Service for Squatters (or A.S.S — no wonder it is a pain for every homeowner who has to deal with them!)

Currently, thanks to this law change in 2012, many of the rights of squatters have been abolished even if they are poor and homeless.

Entering a property for the purpose of residence without permission is now a criminal offence, not a civil one, as was the case in the past. However, this new law does not give the owner the right to evacuate the intruders himself— only the police have the right to do so, under certain conditions.

But despite all these differences with Americans, do not make the mistake of assuming that the British are closer in their customs and traditions to their European neighbours. We should not forget that it is only in the past few decades that have seen relative peace between Britain and Europeans in general. Even so, many English still refer to the French as 'Frogs' (as a kind of mockery, because the French are famous for eating frog legs).[27] No doubt this suspicion contributed to the 2016 Brexit referendum decision, a suspicion excellently lampooned in another episode of the famous Yes, Minister series.[28] The British have always been, and will always be, suspicious of their continental neighbours; as Jim Hacker put it in Yes, Minister: "You know what they say about the average Common Market official? He has the organising ability of the Italians, the flexibility of the Germans, and the modesty of the French. And that's topped up by the imagination of the Belgians, the generosity of the Dutch and the intelligence of the Irish." I'm not quite sure that the scriptwriters would be able to get away with that phraseology in today's climate!

Despite the relative peace across the continent, many may not be aware that the British have fought for more than 15 years with their neighbours when it was still a member of the European Union (EU) over a unified definition – for chocolate! According to the French and Belgians, the name 'chocolate' should not be used to describe British products (such as the famous Cadbury chocolate bars) which

---

27 Suspicion of other cultures and strengthening nationalism were two things that were later exploited by certain parties such as the UK Independence Party (UKIP) who promoted Britain's exit from the European Union in the Brexit referendum of 2016.

28 https://www.politico.eu/article/sir-antony-jay-what-yes-minister-satire-tv-show-taught-us-about-europe/

contain a high percentage of vegetable oils, but only on products manufactured exclusively from cocoa butter.

It did not stop there. Chocolate purists even called for a complete ban on the import of British products until their name was changed. It was only in 2000 that this 'crisis' was resolved, when EU members finally reached a settlement with several provisions, including allowing the use of vegetable fats instead of cocoa butter for up to 5% of the total weight of a chocolate product, as long as this is clearly mentioned on the packaging.[29]

It is true that many Brexiteers today blame the EU for many of the UK's economic and migration problems, but one should not forget that Britain's membership in the EU has contributed to the repeal of some of the country's strangest old laws, such as the 16th-century law prohibiting men from beating their wives after 9pm, not due to anything related to women's rights but because of the inconvenience it caused to neighbours.[30] On the other hand, don't think the old British justice system didn't care for women's rights. In a judgement reported in 1837, a woman was acquitted of biting off a man's nose after he insisted on kissing her against her will.[31]

Finally, if you — perish the thought — decide to die in this Alice-in-Wonderland called the United Kingdom, then it had better not happen within the Houses of Parliament. Allegedly, it is against the law to die within those buildings, although I am not sure what punishment can be imposed on you, if you do![32]

---

29 Source: *BBC News*, May 25th, 2000: Euro Chocolate Wars End": http://news.bbc. co.uk/1/hi/world/europe/764305.stm

30 Source: *The Guardian*, November 28th, 2014:

http://www.theguardian.com/society-professionals/ng-interactive/2014/nov/28/domestic-violence-legislation-timeline.

31 Source: *The Guardian*, 7th May 2011: https://www.theguardian.com/theguardian/from-the-archive-blog/2011/may/07/newspapers-national-newspapers4

32 Source: *The Daily Mirror*, February 3rd, 2002: https://www.mirror.co.uk/news/uk-news/did-you-know-its-illegal-to-die-298718

CHAPTER V

THE GOD DELUSION

For the Adhaan (the Islamic call for prayer chanted five times a day) not to be commonly heard across London was no surprise for me living there. As any regular traveller to Western or non-Muslim countries would tell you, the norm — depending on the country you visit — would be that you typically only hear it either inside the mosque, or publicly in Muslim-majority neighbourhoods or areas.

Of course, this is definitely not the case in major Islamic cities, such as my home town of Jeddah, where the call for prayer is loudly heard and amplified through microphones and speakers. Even a modern Muslim metropolis like Dubai — as cosmopolitan and full of European expats as it is — still regularly plays recordings of the Adhaan inside malls and shopping centres.

Equally muted, dare I say, was the sound of church bells. Even during Sunday services, it was frustrating for me to barely hear the bells toll. Why would it matter to me, an Arab Muslim, you may ask?

Well, apart from the historical and cultural aspects one associates with England, here are a few facts that might surprise you: given that Christians are considered in my religion as fellow 'People of the Book',[1] I actually find comfort in hearing church bells, and enjoy listening to Christian chants (in both Arabic and English), especially around Christmas time.

In fact, in my family, we celebrated Christmas, even before it recently became allowed to do so in Saudi Arabia.[2] You would be right to assume that this was not — and perhaps is still not — that common in Saudi Arabia, or even among Muslims in general, some of whom don't believe that religious celebrations of other faiths should be marked.

But apart from the curiosity and the intrigue, there was another — perhaps spiritual — element to me missing both the sound of the Adhaan, and wishing that church bells were more commonly heard. In both cases, I felt those sounds would have been a reminder that the same God is here, protecting and watching over us, despite being worshipped in two different ways. I know many people — especially in Western societies — might disagree, or find such views old-fashioned or naïve. But these are my views. And while I don't have to justify them, I will say — for argument's sake — that readers must remember that coming from Saudi Arabia, religion has naturally played a big part in my life, even though most of those who know me don't regard me as religious.

The other aspect is that in countries like Egypt, Lebanon and Syria, where many laws are loosely implemented (or absent altogether), God becomes the only refuge for many people. In other words, when people feel that the system doesn't protect them, they pray for justice, or even for revenge against those who did them wrong.

---

1 Muslims respect both Christians and Jews as being People of the Book, that is, people who received revelations from God before the time of Prophet Muhammad and the revelation of the Qur'an, which is God's final Scripture.

2 Under my editorship, and in line with the huge reforms in Saudi Arabia since 2016, the *Arab News* newspaper was the first in the Kingdom to publish a Christmas edition in December 2022. The Crown Prince also met with the Archbishop of Canterbury in 2018 at Lambeth Palace in London.

The United Kingdom, on the other hand, the birthplace of the Magna Carta,[3] is a country renowned worldwide for its courts, legal system and its obsession with justice. Many historical and cultural factors contribute to this sense. Of course, I am not saying British society is ideal, but comparatively speaking, one could argue that the notion of 'cronyism' is virtually non-existent in the British system, or at least it seems to be.

One of the first examples of this I witnessed was the resignation of Home Secretary David Blunkett[4] in December 2004. This was after the Press exposed him for taking advantage of his position to speed up procedures for his former lover to hire a Filipino nanny. Some of my Arab friends are very surprised when I tell them this story, since in many of our countries, the majority of politicians have no shame in taking advantage of their positions to grow their personal wealth. For example, if Blunkett had been a minister in a country like Lebanon, he would have not only used his authority to expedite a nanny visa for his own personal use, but he would have also probably established a private company to recruit domestic workers. Not only that, he would have also introduced monopoly laws forcing the shutdown of his competitors, become rich and ensured that his eldest son inherited both the company and government role.

A similar situation happened with the former British Chancellor of the Exchequer, George Osborne, back in 2012. That year, he made headlines for getting caught boarding a train as a first-class

---

3 Magna Carta or 'The Great Charter': An English document issued for the first time in 1215. The reason for its importance is that it included a waiver by the King of England, granting himself absolute freedom, and a pledge not to punish any 'free man' except under the State's law. This document is of great importance, especially since many laws and constitutions are inspired by it, including the Constitution of the United States.

4 David Blunkett: British politician and academic, born in 1947. He is an inspiration for many Britons because he was born blind and comes from a poor family. He held several ministries during the tenure of Prime Minister Tony Blair, who was also leader of the Labour Party between 2001 and 2005.

passenger while he had booked an economy ticket. Since British ticket inspectors are renowned for not making exceptions for anyone, the minister had to pay the ticket's price difference in addition to a fine for his violation. You only need to compare that to what former Lebanese foreign minister Gebran Bassil publicly said during an interview with CNBC at the 2020 World Economic Forum in Davos. Speaking to then CNBC anchor Hadley Gamble, he bragged about borrowing a friend's private plane to attend the event. His fellow panellist, the Dutch minister Sigrid Kaag, couldn't help herself and said in absolute astonishment: "you wouldn't be allowed to have friends like that in my country."

But be it petty matters, such as a first class train ticket, or major corruption cases pursued by the British Serious Fraud Office,[5] it seems there is no amount of church bells or Muslim calls for prayer that would deter those intending to break the law. This fact, as well as scientific evidence, are among the strongest arguments atheists use to dispute religious beliefs.

As a journalist, I had read a lot about secularism in Europe and had been following the rising tide of atheism. Still, for some reason, I assumed Britain would be different. I realised we were no longer in medieval times and I wasn't exactly expecting the knights of the Crusades to be queuing with me in their shining armour upon my arrival at Heathrow. Still, it is important to keep in mind that Britain is officially a Christian nation, and not a secular one, as some presume. This is still a country ruled by a king — or queen — who officially heads the Anglican Church and holds the title of 'Defender

---

5 The Serious Fraud Office (SFO) is a non-ministerial British government department, formed in 1988, which is tasked with pursuing the most important cases of fraud. In Saudi Arabia, we have an equivalent organisation called Nazaha, the National Anti-Corruption Commission.

of Faith',[6] so I guess one can be excused for making at least a tiny assumption.

Yet, the reality check came in much faster than I had imagined. The cover of the first issue of Newsweek I saw in my hotel room on my first night in London read: "Is There Room for God in a Secular Europe?"[7] As a journalist from Saudi Arabia, it wouldn't be an overstatement to say I was taken by the audacity of the cover at the time. While it was okay for Saudi media to discuss secularism or atheism during that period, it was — and perhaps still is — a taboo in most Arab countries to wonder whether there was 'room for God' in the Middle East.

Yet this was nothing compared to what I stumbled upon next. Suddenly, a magazine cover questioning if there was space left for the Almighty on the continent didn't seem so shocking two years later, when a whole book came out to doubt His existence altogether! I am referring, of course, to the debate which erupted in Britain around the controversial book, The God Delusion. Within just months, this became one of the best-selling books of 2006,[8] despite the anger it sparked among devout people of all religions.

In this book, British biologist — and obviously atheist — Richard Dawkins claims that there is actually no creator of the universe with supernatural powers. He also argues that a person does not need to be religious to be morally committed. And it seems many agree with Mr Dawkins. According to the 2021 British census, while Christianity

---

6 The Defender of Faith is one of the titles given to the kings of England and they still hold it till this day. King Henry VIII was the first to bear the title, on October 11, 1521, when Pope Leo X granted it to him in recognition of his stance in support of the Pope's holiness, the institution of marriage and in opposition to the Protestant revolution in its early stages. However, Pope Paul III withdrew the title from King Henry when the latter decided to separate from Rome and appoint himself as the head of the Anglican Church in 1530. But he regained the title when the English Parliament voted in 1544 to grant King Henry, and all his successors, the title of defender of the Christian Anglican faith.

7 *Newsweek* magazine, European edition, November 8, 2004: Soul Searching: is There Room for God in a Secular Europe?

8 The book, in its English version, had sold more than 3 million copies by September 2014.

(in all its sects) remains the majority religion with 46%, the second official 'religion' in the UK is 'no-religion' (whether it is complete atheism, or just not following any religion), with a rate of 37%. More importantly, the vast majority (65%) of those who classify themselves as 'Christians' also describe themselves as 'not religious', while 79% of those surveyed believe that "religion is the origin of wars and misery that the world is experiencing today".[9]

On the other hand, I confess that many of us Arabs go too far in our obsession with the occult, or conversations about the supernatural. It is surreal to have people among us who have attended the best universities, travelled the world and are leading modern lives, but at the same time still visit fortune-tellers and base their life decisions on their predictions!

Nevertheless, I was shocked to discover that Britons are not much better. For instance, according to a recent study,[10] one out of every three Britons believes in ghosts, and 39% believe that homes may be haunted by evil spirits, while 9% claim that they were able to communicate with the dead!

Since we mentioned death, I must say that there are striking differences that emerge when comparing the British culture to the Arab-Muslim culture in which I was raised. For example, graves in our culture fill us with a sense of awe. The issue of retribution after death, which some of us believe begins once a person is buried, is a constant concern for many. Here is an idea of what some are taught — in school, at home, and in the mosque — about what comes after death: A person's grave narrows or expands according to their deeds. So, the grave narrows if the sins of the deceased overshadow their good deeds and an iron hammer falls on their heads. But, if their

9 These figures are based on the official survey conducted in the United Kingdom — National Census UK — for the year 2021, which also showed that Islam is the fourth religion in the country, at 6.5%. https://www.ons.gov.uk/peoplepopulationandcommunity/culturalidentity/religion/bulletins/religionenglandandwales/census2021

10 A study by YouGov, a global public opinion and data company, issued in 2014. https://yougov.co.uk/politics/articles/10857-ghosts-exist-say-1-3-brits

good deeds are abundant, the grave will expand and a beam of light gleaming from the sky will show them their seat in Paradise.

With all that in mind, you can only imagine how awkward the scene was when I used to walk by a graveyard every day for nearly five years on my way to and from my new flat in Fulham. The graveyard was called Brompton Cemetery, and it used to be a park.[11] Each and every time I walked between Earl's Court Station and my flat, I always looked the other way and distracted myself with music from my iPod (although I am a big Michael Jackson fan, Thriller was definitely not on the playlist!)[12]

Yet, you can imagine how surreal it was for me, when I actually dared to look into the cemetery, to see British men and women going for their morning jogs between the tombs, in sweatpants and listening to music with a look of determination in their eyes that read: "I am going to burn that holiday weight off, no matter what." On the opposite side, sat some of my less health-obsessed neighbours, indulging in cupcakes and lattes in cute little coffee shops that had 'a view to die for' overseeing the cemetery!

It turns out that according to several online guides to the best running areas in London, this particular cemetery was among the highest recommended places, due to its 'scenic greenery' and 'vast landscape'. As I researched this book, I tried to ask these joggers if they found what they were doing problematic. Some made it clear to me, in a rather patronising way, that they were not jogging on the graves themselves, but on the paths between them. Others tried to explain it to me in a different way, saying:

"If people are not bothered by us jogging in between their homes in residential neighbourhoods while they are still alive, then why would

---

11 In 1840 the British Parliament issued a decision to convert this park into a public cemetery.

12 *Thriller* was released in the UK in 1983 and has appeared on the global Billboard Hot 100 chart many times. The video which accompanied it featured zombies dancing.

they be disturbed by us doing so when they're dead?"

My phobia of walking by the cemetery naturally increased in the evening. And even more so in winter, when the night falls earlier, the trees become bare and the cold wind blows. While I used to rush, trying to think about anything other than the cemetery to get past it in the fastest possible time, you can only imagine how stunned I was at the sight of two teenagers passionately kissing in front of its gate! However, an English friend of mine explained this phenomenon to me, and the mystery was solved:

"When you are 16 or 17 and you want to get comfortable kissing a girl without any of your parents or neighbours seeing you...where else do you take her?"

There is also another fascinating story in that regard that must be told. I was studying for my Master's degree at the University of Westminster in London,[13] when my Professor of Direct Marketing — a very kind, elderly Englishwoman who owned twelve cats (and just had to talk about them during every lecture) — brought a letter that she had once received and read it to us, as an example of how marketing managers chose their target audience wisely. From what I remember of the letter she received from the funeral services office in her neighbourhood, it read:

"According to our database, you will be reaching retirement age soon, so we decided to present you with a special offer to book your funeral with us in advance for a chance to get a 20% discount and free wreaths, thus saving costs for your loved ones later."

Of course — as is normal with the British people — my lecturer

---

13 I attended university between 2007 and 2009 and chose to take evening classes. I will discuss the details of this experience in an upcoming chapter called *A Study in Scarlet.*

mocked herself and the situation after reading the text and said jokingly:

> *"Well, now I can say that if I did not teach you anything during my life, at least you will learn something from my death!"*

****

When I spoke earlier in this chapter about how muted church bells were in London, that certainly did not include the ancient and iconic churches such as Westminster Abbey and St. Paul's Cathedral. In addition to their religious significance, these historical buildings are also prominent tourist attractions that captivate thousands of visitors daily. Those who look after the buildings are mindful of holding religious prayers and ceremonies in addition to taking care of their maintenance and preservation as an unparalleled cultural heritage in the world.[14]

Nevertheless, not all churches in Britain — especially if they are smaller or less important — enjoy the same support and donations that keep them going. The number of churches has diminished due to the decline in religiosity (as mentioned earlier). Therefore, it is very common to come across an advertisement in daily newspapers promoting the sale or rent of an unused church.

While there are churches that have been converted into homes, dance schools, supermarkets, bookshops and temples for other religions, some have controversially been turned into bars and

---

14 It is worth noting that both churches depend entirely and exclusively on selling tickets to visitors and on fundraisers, as they do not receive any support or allocations from the government nor the King.

nightclubs.[15] Perhaps the most famous case is the Irish pub O'Neills in Muswell Hill, north London, which was once a church of great architectural beauty (built in 1902), but today is now a place "in which nothing but beer is worshipped".[16]

In another pub, I asked a random Englishman how he felt about using churches for purposes other than worship. He replied:

"If you ask the landlord, he will tell you that he does not mind converting the building back to a place of worship...as long as God is willing to pay the rent!"

At that moment, I expected to hear thunder erupting and this indecent fellow suddenly struck by lightning as punishment for his blasphemy. Because of my upbringing, and what I learned about religion and its sanctity, it bothered me when religion or religious figures were insulted. (To be fair, many Arabs — especially in Iraq and the Levant — are infamous for swearing and cursing God and religion as part of their daily conversations. This is not done out of lack of faith but is really just an extremely vulgar way to emphasise their frivolity and manliness.)[17] As for the Englishman in the pub, he probably didn't regard what he said as obscene or offensive. I

---

15 Source: *Daily Mail*, 29th February 2024: https://www.dailymail.co.uk/property/ article-13135725/religious-conversions-Churches-UK-saved-dereliction-turned-night-clubs-bars-university.html#:~:text=REAL%20religious%20conversions!-,Churches%20 across%20UK%20are%20saved%20from%20dereliction%20by%20being,night-clubs%2C%20bars%20and%20university%20digs&text=Churches%20across%20 the%20UK%20are,are%20turning%20away%20from%20religion.

It is also worth noting that there are laws regulating the conversion and the use of churches in Britain. Any sacred icon or emblem must be removed, and the building cannot be used as a sex shop, or as a casino where there would be gambling.

16 Source: Getty Images https://www.gettyimages.ie/detail/news-photo/picture-shows-the-bar-at-oneills-pub-in-a-former-news-photo/465149511

17 What is ironic is that many of these 'cursers' and slanderers participate in angry protests when a Western media outlet publishes an article or a cartoon that offends Islam, for example.

also think he assumed that as long as he was talking about his own religion — and not mine — that it would be acceptable.

Nevertheless, my observations of British society must not lead you to believe that faith has completely vanished from Britain; actually there are still many religious and practising people. Among them are those who certainly resent what is happening to churches, while many of them still passionately preach Christianity, but of course using more modern and less intrusive methods.

One night, as I was riding the bus home late, a passenger of African descent (which I could tell by his colourful clothes and Bob Marley look) surprised me by asking me if I was facing any problems.

I told him: "Yes, we all have problems."

So, he said with a smile: "Okay, let me introduce you to a friend who helped me with all my problems."

Then, this long and curly haired young man began to chant a beautiful song about Jesus, whose lyrics said, "I love that man!" and asked me to sing along. I respectfully declined by saying: "Well, I do love that man, but I need to get off here."

There are also some volunteers who befriend Arab tourists on Edgware Road, distributing an Arabic copy of the Bible printed in such a way as to disguise it to look like a copy of the Qur'an. You can listen to preachers (not just Christians, but of all faiths) preaching every week at Speakers' Corner[18] in Hyde Park, or sometimes debating one another.

Since we are talking about the religiousness of some Britons, I witnessed a remarkable event on January 8th, 2005, while I was visiting the BBC's building in White City, west of London. While I was about to enter the building, I was startled by an angry protest carried out by dozens of people criticising the BBC's decision to

---

18 Contrary to popular belief, no-one is free to say whatever they want at Speakers' Corner. This spot is subject to the same laws in force throughout the United Kingdom (except in the Parliament where speakers have immunity), regarding offensiveness. For example, full nudity is prohibited and so is defaming and insulting people.

broadcast a satirical television play called Jerry Springer — The Opera.[19]

The protesters considered that the play offended Christianity and what it stands for, as it insulted and mocked Jesus and raised doubts about his sexual orientation. The protesters chanted angrily as they burned copies of their TV Licence[20] bills:

"What do we want?... Jerry Springer, out! When do we want it?... Now!"

Because I was still working as a journalist for *Asharq al-Awsat* newspaper at the time, I immediately took the initiative to take pictures and notes.[21] I remember an angry lady telling me that she spoke for "all Christians in Britain" when I asked her why she didn't simply refrain from watching the play, instead of demanding to stop it:

"If it was less offensive, we wouldn't be so angry and would settle for not watching it".

This 50-year-old woman explained that the reason for her frustration

---

19 This is a British musical written by Richard Thomas and Stewart Lee which lampoons the American talk show host Jerry Springer.

20 A TV licence is a tax imposed by the British government on every home that watches or records television broadcasts, whether it is local, international, or through cable and the Internet. Tax evasion or failure to pay is a crime punishable by law with a penalty that might go as far as imprisonment. It is noteworthy that the earnings from this tax go to fund the channels and platforms of the British Broadcasting Corporation (BBC) so that it is an outlet that serves the public and is not subject to a commercial agenda (no commercial advertisements are accepted) nor a government agenda (because the funding does not come from the government but from taxpayer money directly).

21 My coverage of this protest was published under the title 'Controversial TV Show ignites Demonstrations in Front of BBC Building in London' in *Asharq al-Awsat* newspaper on January 8, 2005. http://archive.aawsat.com/details.asp?section=4&issueno=9538&article=276113&search=%DD%ED%D5%E1%20%DA%C8%C7%D3&state=true#. WL-y9nS6mf0

was that the BBC insisted on broadcasting the play, despite receiving 15,000 petitions. As a result of the protest, the BBC decided to postpone the show until late at night, and also made sure to broadcast several warnings that the content might be disturbing for some.

The moral of this story is that the protesters obtained part of their demands, so they were able to limit what they considered to be the negative impact of this play. But at the same time, they did not break the law in the name of religion because they were not able to get their full demands.

Perhaps one of the striking paradoxes — at least for me — is that exactly ten years after the occurrence of this protest, which ended peacefully, and achieved part of what the protesters sought, a horrific terrorist incident occurred against another media outlet in the French capital, Paris.

On January 7th, 2015, two terrorists who said they were part of Al-Qaeda in Yemen stormed the offices of the French satirical magazine *Charlie Hebdo*, which many deemed was providing dreadful and provocative content. The attackers carried out a massacre — in the name of religion — that killed eleven journalists and a policeman and injured eleven others, in retaliation for this magazine publishing disgusting cartoons about the Prophet Muhammad (which I absolutely think was both wrong and unnecessarily provocative).

When we come to compare the results, we find that the protest carried out in London against Jerry Springer — The Opera was more effective, as it limited the number of viewers that night. And because they did not commit any violent acts, the show did not gain any further fame and I doubt anyone remembers it at all today.

As for the case of Charlie Hebdo, thanks to the crimes of these two murderers, dozens of newspapers and magazines around the world have shared their cartoons. Therefore, all that the two perpetrators were able to achieve was to increase restrictions imposed on millions of innocent Muslims in Europe and contribute to further distort the image of Islam.

Chapter VI

CAPTAIN HOOK

Wednesday, July 6th, 2005, was a long and exciting day for Britain. Londoners were mostly glued to their TV sets, be it at home or in their offices. This was the long-awaited day the results were to be announced determining which city was to host the 2012 Olympic games. Adding to the suspense was the historical rivalry between the contenders: it was The City of Lights (Paris) vs. The City of Fog (London).

London had been preparing for this moment since 1997, when the British Olympic Association started assembling its bid. Pulling no punches, the Association relied on the 'celebrity endorsement' of Prince William, football legend David Beckham and (then) Prime Minister, Tony Blair. The stakes were high, as winning would not only cement London's position as a global city, but would also coincide with the Diamond Jubilee of (now late) Queen Elizabeth II's accession to the throne.[1]

---

1 Queen Elizabeth II acceded to the throne on February 6th, 1952. In 2012, she became the only British Queen, aside from Queen Victoria, to spend sixty years on the British throne.

At last, the International Olympic Committee reached a verdict: the winner was indeed London. As the decision was announced live on television channels, Londoners of all ethnicities, religions and walks of life took to the streets, waved British flags, cheered and toasted their drinks to mark the wonderful win.

However, that happy moment did not last long! The next morning, as the British capital was still sobering up after a long night of celebrations, four terrorists blew themselves up on board three Underground trains and a crowded bus in central London. Amid the overwhelming chaos and uncertainty that prevailed, nobody realised that Britain had just witnessed the most violent terrorist attack since the Lockerbie incident[2] in 1988, and the first suicide attack in its history.

Just like the September 11th, 2001, terrorist attacks are now referred to as 9/11 in the United States, the events which took place in London that day, which left 52 dead and more than 700 injured, have widely become known as the 7/7 Attacks.

At the time (in 2005), social media was not as widespread as it is today. Therefore, most people, especially those who were not in central London, where the attacks took place, did not find out what had happened till later on. As for me, I felt that something was wrong when I arrived at the Hanger Lane Underground station (where I was living for a brief period of time) on my way to work. The station was shut down and completely empty, except for one employee who stood at the entrance to inform all inquirers that they needed to avoid going to central London because the transport network was completely down.

---

2 The Lockerbie incident: on December 21st, 1988, a bomb on board a Pan Am airplane exploded above the Scottish village of Lockerbie. The incident lead to the death of all 243 passengers and 16 crew members that were on board the plane, in addition to 11 other people who were killed when the plane fell to the ground. Years of investigation found that Libya had a hand in the incident. In 2003, the Libyan leader Muammar Gaddafi assumed responsibility for the attack (he did not however say that it took place based on his orders, despite the fact that his former Justice Minister Mustafa Abdul Jalil later said otherwise) and compensation was paid to the families of the victims.

Nobody was quite sure what was going on until the security correspondent of the British Broadcasting Corporation (BBC), Frank Gardner,[3] went live on a newscast to say that his sources had confirmed that what had happened in London was a terrorist operation, perpetrated by Al-Qaeda: the same terrorist organisation which had planned and executed the 9/11 attacks in America four years earlier.

Undoubtedly, this was a pivotal moment for me, whether as an international journalist living in London who knew right there and then that this story would dominate the headlines for years to come; or as an immigrant Muslim residing in Britain who feared the repercussions that these attacks might have in terms of consequent discrimination and hate crimes.

However, my fears quickly vanished. Instead, I found myself acknowledging for the first time, with complete conviction, that this country is truly great. This was thanks to the carefully selected, sincere and reassuring words that were spoken by the head of London's Metropolitan Police at the time, Sir Ian Blair. Speaking live during a televised press conference shortly after the attacks, Sir Ian gave a highly responsible and admirable answer to a very loaded question when he was asked whether he considered it was 'Islamic terrorism' which was behind that morning's attacks. The veteran officer calmly responded by saying that it was important to differentiate between the two words, as there was something called 'terrorism' and another called 'Islam' and there was no inevitable correlation between the two.

Obviously, such a mature and calculated response was very different

---

3 Frank Gardner is a British journalist specialising in the affairs of the Middle East and the fight against terrorism. In 2004, while he was on a journalistic mission to cover the Saudi war against terrorism, Gardner was shot at by supporters of Al-Qaeda in Al-Suwaidi neighbourhood in the Saudi Capital, Riyadh. The attack left Gardner paralysed, while the Irish cameraman accompanying him, Simon Cumbers, was killed. It should be noted that the Saudi authorities arrested the perpetrator of the attack and later executed him on January 2nd, 2016.

to what had happened in America a few years before: former US President George W. Bush stated after 9/11 that he was fighting a new 'crusade'. His words were seen as a statement against Islam as a whole and gave cover to a really atrocious period for American Muslims who had nothing to do with Al Qaeda.

Yet, because there is no good deed that goes unpunished, terrorists chose to test British tolerance again less than two weeks later and launched similar attacks in central London on July 21st, 2005 (causing no casualties). Once more, the British government insisted on containing the issue and dealing with its repercussions with a combination of private firmness and public calmness. While special forces and anti-terrorism squads were investigating and arresting suspects, other officials worked in parallel to ensure that the daily lives of the millions residing in the capital city went on uninterrupted.

This resulted in life returning to normal in London within just a few days, in line with the famous British saying: 'Keep Calm and Carry on.'[4]

Of course, while one must acknowledge that Britain is not free of racism or hate crimes, I can only talk about my personal experience. I personally have never experienced any racism from any Briton during my time in London, whether before or after the events of 7/7. This applies to both private citizens and public officials and is supported by the fact that the British government has policies in place that

---

4 *Keep Calm and Carry On* is a poster campaign that was launched by the British government in 1939 in preparation for the Second World War. It aimed at lifting the spirits of the British people, who were at risk of air raids. Despite the fact that more than two million posters were actually made at the time and that many British cities were bombarded, these posters were not widely distributed. The campaign did not become known until the year 2000, when one of the posters was discovered in a library. Today, the phrase is being used again as part of the contemporary British culture in various campaigns.

reject all forms of discrimination[5] — whether on the basis of race, gender or religion.

Was I just lucky? Perhaps. Maybe it was my profession, or the circles I frequented, which meant that I — by default — spent time with open-minded, worldly people. Needless to say, I have read many stories about racism. There is no doubt that some white supremacists practice racism — even violence sometimes — against blacks, Asians (such as use of the term 'Paki' as referenced by Azeem Rafiq),[6] Jews, Arabs and Muslims. So I understand that the opposite of my own experience is also true.

Racism even occurs among white people themselves, such as the abuse directed towards Polish immigrants who came in waves to work in Britain after their country joined the European Union in 2004. On the other hand, racism and hate crimes also occur between the minorities themselves, such as some incidents that involved Muslims and Jews for example, typically fuelled by events that take place in Israel and the Occupied Palestinian Territories. The most recent waves of antisemitism, Islamophobia and hate attacks followed on from the 7th October 2023 attacks.

However, I do believe such incidents are exceptions, and are temporary. It is nearly impossible, in accordance with the laws currently in force, for any racist or discriminatory practice to last for a long time. Perhaps one of most prominent examples would be

---

5 In 1965, the Race Relations Act was adopted, making racial discrimination in public places an offence. This was followed by two laws adopted in 1968 and 1976, which banned discrimination in the areas of housing, employment and public services. In 1998, the United Kingdom joined, with the entirety of its institutions, the European Convention on Human Rights.

6 Azeem Rafiq is a former professional cricketer who spent the majority of his career at Yorkshire. He was born in Pakistan and moved to England when he was 10 years old. He captained England at youth level and eventually became captain of Yorkshire in 2012. In September 2020, he gave an interview to *ESPN Cricinfo*, in which he claimed that "institutional racism" at Yorkshire County Cricket Club had left him close to taking his own life.

obliging the far-right British National Party (BNP)[7] to change its working system, which, before the case reached the courts in 2009, limited the party's membership to 'indigenous Caucasians' only.

You might think this positive view of Britain is understandable coming from a declared Anglophile. But it is definitely not only that. It is an opinion that is backed by many facts and real examples. How can anyone accuse a nation of racism or discrimination when its Archbishop praises Islamic values publicly and on several occasions? I refer to Dr. Rowan Williams, who was the Archbishop of Canterbury between 2002 and 2012.

Dr Williams actually had to face a wave of criticism during his time as Archbishop when he suggested the inclusion of some aspects of the Sharia law in the British law, giving British Muslims the option of referring to the Sharia judiciary in several cases such as divorce, financial dealings and conflict resolution.

On the other hand, I find it surreal that many of those who accuse the British of being racist are unbelievably intolerant and racist themselves. Discriminatory practices in many Arab countries are widespread and are not limited to religious aspects. Lebanon — and I say this comfortably given that I do have Lebanese roots — is probably among the worst Arab countries on this front. And why would one expect the Lebanese not to be as such when their whole political system and wealth distribution is based on sectarianism and subsequent quotas? As it stands now, only a Christian Maronite can become President, only a Sunni Muslim can become Prime Minister and only a Shiite can become Speaker of Parliament.

As such, it is not surprising to learn that 'Russians', for example, is a word used by the Lebanese to refer to all female sex workers, whether

---

7 The British National Party was established in 1982 and was characterised by its racist stance against non-white people. One of its most controversial positions was proposing the adoption of a voluntary programme to send migrants and their children back to their places of origin. This party also called for the return of capital punishment to Britain, opposed the right of gay people to get married and was one of the greatest opponents of what it describes as the 'Islamisation' of the United Kingdom.

they are Russian or not. Meanwhile, 'Sri Lankan' is used to refer to all housemaids, while Abeed (or 'slaves' in English) was an awful word used until recently to refer to people with black skin.[8] The level of discrimination even reaches the point where some beach resorts prohibit the entry of housemaids, whether they are accompanying the families they work with or coming alone, due to racist reasons related to their ethnicities (and regardless whether they are Filipino, Ethiopian or Sri Lankan...Sri Lankans!).[9]

On the other hand, such matters are taken very seriously in Britain, where the country currently has a Prime Minister of Indian origins (Rishi Sunak), a Mayor of London of Pakistani roots (Sadiq Khan) and a black Home Secretary (James Cleverly). British courtrooms regularly deal with discrimination cases. Examples of this abound: a telephone service employee of Indian descent sued his company for firing him after he refused to use an alternative English name (so that clients could communicate with him easily). Similarly, a bank employee in his forties successfully sued his bank for replacing him with a younger employee, while many years ago, two gay men successfully sued a small hotel because the receptionist refused to rent them a room together... and so on!

Muslims too fought similar legal battles and won on several occasions. For example, a hijab-wearing hairdresser received compensation of £4,000 when she filed a lawsuit against the owner of a female salon that refused to hire because she covered her hair, which the owner claimed would interfere with her ability to do her job.[10]

In 2013, two Muslim employees won a lawsuit against a Tesco

---

8 Local manufacturer Gandour in the 1950s began selling a chocolate marshmallow called Ras El Abd, which meant 'Slave's Head.' The name was recently changed to Tarboosh (Fez) but the original name is still used by locals.

9 Source: the BBC website, August 13th, 2009 – http://news.bbc.co.uk/2/hi/8200001.stm

10 Source: the BBC Website, June 16th, 2008 – http://news.bbc.co.uk/2/hi/uk_news/england/london/7457794.stm

supermarket branch because the managers of the store installed a lock on the door of the prayer room, insisted on it remaining closed outside of prayer times and asked the employees wishing to use it to sign a logsheet when entering and leaving the room.[11]

Of course, there are also several incidents where the British went unreasonably too far in their quest for inclusion and political correctness to the extent they were tolerant to some incredibly intolerant people. For example, some British Muslims oppose others using the word 'Christmas' to describe the holiday which marks the birth of Christ on 25th December. They argue that this religious occasion celebrated by the majority of this Christian country should be referred to as the 'winter holiday'. Needless to say, this is both ridiculous and unacceptable. I am glad that that, ultimately, the Muslim Council of Britain[12] launched a campaign to clarify that this opinion only represents a small minority and that most Muslims do not see this celebration as a form of discrimination or an insult at all.[13]

***

An interesting story happened to me when I went with my newspaper colleague and dear friend, Hatem Oweida, to produce a feature about the Birmingham Central Mosque in September 2005. Hatem is British of Palestinian origins and was the paper's senior photographer at the time.

Birmingham, located in Britain's West Midlands, is characterised

---

11 Source: the *Daily Mail*, October 3rd, 2013 – http://www.dailymail.co.uk/news/article-2442448/Muslim-Tesco-workers-win-discrimination-case-bosses-locked-prayer-room.html.

12 The Muslim Council of Britain (MCB) is body that was established in 1997 and includes 500 mosques, schools and Islamic institutions in Britain. It works on raising awareness about the Islamic faith and reducing discrimination and hate speech directed towards Muslims.

13 The posters and messages used in the campaign are posted on the official website on the Muslim Council of Britain http://www.mcb.org.uk/keep-calm-christmas

by several things including that fact that it was an important industrial hub at an important time and is today the second most populated British city with over one million inhabitants. However, the main reason behind the visit was that the city, at the time, used to have 150,000 Muslim residents, or ten percent of the 1.5 million Muslims residing in Britain. In addition, it was the home town of Yassine Hassan Omar (a Brit of Somali decent), who was one of the people under arrest for planning the 21st July 2005 failed terrorist attacks in London.

Having not left London since I arrived, I was surprised by my first impressions of Birmingham. It was very different from what I imagined a major British city would look like. Despite the greenery, the black cabs and red brick buildings, you quickly realise that the English, both in terms of language and ethnicity, are a minority here. Indeed, the majority of people I saw were of Asian decent, and most store fronts had signs in Urdu, in addition to the crescent and star found on the Pakistani flag.

In most of the areas I visited in Birmingham, the outfits worn by people were almost identical: most men had long beards and wore *kufias* on their heads and *Shalwar Kameez* outfits.[14] As for women, most of them wore black Burqas or Hijabs. So dominant was the Asian presence that the sight of one white, blonde lady walking on the street seemed out of place in one neighbourhood.

Had I been a member of the BNP (mentioned earlier) or the English Defence League,[15] I suppose I would have probably fainted at the sight. But I was an Arab Muslim and I was familiar with what I saw and actually rather enjoyed the warmth and friendliness of the people I met. To me, it was yet another sign of how tolerant and welcoming Britain was.

---

14 The traditional Pakistani costume which consists of loose trousers and a long shirt which goes over them.

15 A far-right Islamophobic organisation which formed in 2009 to create disturbances on the streets.

Journalistically, what was interesting to note was the public affirmation of the Islamic identity that you could see everywhere, quite possibly in a way I had never seen so exaggerated before. Almost all of Birmingham's restaurants used the logo 'Halal'. This was not just limited to Pakistani or Indian restaurants. It even included restaurants that served pizza and American-style fried chicken. Needless to say, I had some of the best curry, tandoori chicken and mango lassi that I have ever tried in my life in Birmingham. There were also shops that sold 'Islamic clothing' (robes for men and abayas and head covers for women) and 'Islamic' libraries, the content of which I expected to be limited to translated Qurans and prayer booklets along with manuals explaining how to perform religious duties, such as Hajj and Umrah, and so on.

However, there was an element of surprise there. I had not expected to find books and films that incited hate, and warning of what they called the 'new Crusaders' with the flags of both the UK and the US adorning them. There were also t-shirts and coffee mugs with slogans like 'I am God's Lion' and 'Victory for Islam' written on them. Again, all this was taking place publicly and comfortably, weeks after the 7/7 attacks and two years after the Iraq War which Britain played a vital role in. I later wrote that story in detail for *Asharq Al-Awsat* newspaper.[16]

When my colleague Hatem and I arrived at the Central Mosque, after acquiring prior approval to enter it and take photos inside, we were lucky to find a group of elderly white English women, who were on a cultural visit to the mosque to learn the principles of Islam.

Excited about the contrast in the image, Hatem rapidly drew his camera and started taking pictures of the delegation as he moved around, greeted those present and chatted with them. I was busy examining the books and observing the worshippers. I was surprised by a skinny young man in his late teens, who had a beard that reached

---

16 Source: *Asharq Al-Awsat*, September 30th, 2005 – http://archive.aawsat.com/details.asp?article=325869%issueno=9803#.V7B0QvI97z4

the bottom of his neck, yelling at Hatem and threatening him:

"If you take a picture of me, there will be problems!"

I immediately intervened and asked him what was bothering him. He surprised us by saying that he did not want to talk or answer any questions and scolded us, saying: "Taking pictures is haram" (religiously forbidden). Hatem instantly responded by saying: "How can you say this? Didn't you watch Friday Eid prayers that are broadcast live on the telly from Makkah?" but instead of calming down, the young man became angrier and told us: "Do you really believe that these American allies (meaning Saudis) represent true Islam?"

It became obvious at that moment that the young man was trying to create a problem to justify expelling or assaulting us. So I asked Hatem to put the camera aside and I explained to the young man that we were there based on an authorisation given to us by the Mosque's administration. I also added that, in order to avoid any problems, I would go to the administration again and inform them of his objection. He did not reply, gave us a dirty look and walked away.

I went to meet the Mosque's administrator, a bearded, older, chubbier and much more joyful person. He laughed upon hearing the story, downplayed the situation and told me that he would talk to the young man who he described as just 'overzealous'. I asked to meet with the Mosque's Imam to ask about the reason why there was, among the worshippers, someone who believed that taking pictures was haram. To my surprise, the administrator informed me that I couldn't talk to the Imam…because he did not speak Arabic.

I replied by saying: "All right, but as you can see, I can speak English fluently. So, what is the problem?"

"The problem is that he does not speak English either!" he answered with a big smile.

The administrator asked another Imam called Sheikh Talha Bukhari (an equally pleasant man of Asian origins) to talk to me.

He seemed tolerant and assured me that any misconceptions are immediately corrected and that there was no problem with taking pictures as long as it was for good purposes.

On the train back to London, I could not stop thinking about the background and repercussions of what had just happened. Even if the claim that the Imam did not speak English was true (and I have no reason to believe it was not), this still presented a major problem. It meant that a top religious authority in the second largest British city did not speak the main language of the country he was living in. It was therefore not possible for us to believe that he was fully informed about the events and debates taking place around him.

The question that was widely asked in the years following the 7/7 attacks was: "Who speaks for Islam in Britain?" I personally wished for the answer to be limited to moderate Imams. However, I started to notice a near media unanimity, including some prominent institutions, in terms of only hosting the most radical Imams in a bid to stir up controversy.

For example, the British Broadcasting Corporation (BBC) hosted a Ma'zoon[17] to respond to the statements made by Archbishop Rowan Williams, when he called for British law to include some aspects of the Islamic Sharia law.

Instead of praising the gesture of the highest English Christian authority, and pledging to work closely to spread a spirit of tolerance, the Ma'zoon went for an own goal! You can imagine the audience's reaction when this bearded, not-so-happy looking man considered that Islamic Sharia was the only thing that would save British society. When the host asked him why he believed that, the sheikh answered:

"Because if we look, for example, at the ratio of women to men, we will notice that it is 4 to 1... So, if each man marries one woman, three women will remain unmarried. This means that they will become either lesbians or prostitutes."

---

17 The Ma'zoon is a Muslim marriage registrar.

What this Ma'zoon said was not only horrific, but also completely inaccurate as the ratio of women to men he mentioned (4 to 1) was not true at all.[18]

As for the reaction of the teenager we met at the Birmingham Central Mosque, it was obvious that it was a reaction prevailing among many young Muslims when discussing a matter which they felt undermined their religion, just like the angry reactions which occurred when the possible banning of the Burqa was discussed in Britain in 2006.[19]

I don't mean to belittle young people's fervour over their religion and their right to express their views to defend it. As mentioned in the previous chapter, I also reported on British Christians who protested outside the BBC to try and ban a comedy which was demeaning to Jesus Christ. However, I felt that young man in the mosque was an easy target to be manipulated into violence. If he was this angry at — and threatened by — me, a fellow Muslim, what would he have done to a non-Muslim if pushed or incited to do so by a religious figure?

There might not be, in British contemporary history, an inciter who is more infamous than hate preacher Abu Hamza Al-Masri, who is currently serving a life sentence in a US prison after he was extradited there from Britain in 2012. Among the charges brought against the radical preacher in US courts was an accusation of taking part in planning international terrorist attacks, holding hostages, and establishing training camps for fighters. What is interesting about the story of Kamel Mustafa (the real name of Abu Hamza), who was born in Alexandria, Egypt in 1958, is definitely the period he spent as an Imam at Finsbury Park Mosque, located in eastern London, between 1997 and 2003. There, right under the nose and protection of the

---

18 The actual ratio is almost at 1 to 1. According to a 2011 survey, there were 31 million men and 32 million women.

19 Source: *Asharq Al-Awsat*, October 29th, 2006 – http://archive.aawsat.com/details. asp?section=37&issueno=10197&article=389487&search=%C7%E1%E4%DE%C7%C8 &state=true#.V7CWIfl97Z4

British police, he was openly promoting hate and publicly inciting violence. Among his controversial activities was the organisation of a conference on the first anniversary of the September 11th attacks, in which he praised the attacks.

What is remarkable is that it was later found that a significant number of people accused of terrorism had attended the sermons of Abu Hamza at some point. Among those were three of the perpetrators of the 7/7 attacks in London, in addition to the Moroccan-French Zacarias Moussaoui (nicknamed the 'Twentieth Hijacker in the attacks of September 11th), and the British terrorist Richard Reid or the 'shoe bomber', who planned to detonate a bomb on board a passenger plane headed towards Miami from Paris in 2001 and failed.

Security agencies were not the only ones interested in monitoring Abu Hamza — British tabloids found him a particularly 'sexy' topic. In fact, one could argue that for nearly two decades, he was the fiercest competitor to British glamour girls when it came to frontpages, spreads and column inches of papers such as *The Sun, The Daily Mail* and *The Daily Express*. While the supermodels boasted their perfectly carved figures and posed semi-nude in topless photos, Abu Hamza had other body parts to show off. Tabloid editors nicknamed him Captain Hook, Hooky or simply Hook in reference to the metal hook he wore on his right hand. Abu Hamza had lost both his hands and one of his eyes in an incident that took place when he joined the Afghan jihadists in the 1980s.

Most Brits know Captain Hook as the fictional, evil pirate in the famous classical children's story Peter Pan.[20] In the classic, made popular by Disney, the bearded pirate also lost one of his hands and

---

20 *Peter Pan* is a children's story written by the Scottish novelist James Matthew Barrie. It focuses on the adventures lived by a child named Peter, who does not grow up and can fly, on the fictional island 'Neverland'. Throughout these adventures, Peter receives the help of his friends, mainly Tinker Bell, the small fairy that makes wishes come true. He also faces villains such as Captain Hook, the pirate with a missing hand, which he replaced with a metal hook. The novel was published in many forms and various languages. What mainly contributed to its spread was Walt Disney turning it into a cartoon movie in 1953.

replaced it with a metal hook. As you can imagine, it did not take long
— thanks to this analogy — for Abu Hamza to become well known
as a hateful person, with his hideous statements, untrimmed beard
and unconventional clothes. Due to his injuries, he was classified by
the NHS as a person with special needs, so he benefitted for years
from assistance provided by the State. The assistance included a large
five-bedroom house for his family of eight people, which was until
recently worth £1.25 million. This comes in addition to the financial
assistance, estimated at £33,000 every year, from which his family
still benefits.[21]

Needless to say, all this came at the expense of British taxpayers.
The same taxpayers also had to incur a cost estimated at £30,000
every year for a nurse, whose job was to clean Abu Hamza's derrière
after he used the bathroom. This took place during the time he
was imprisoned in Britain between 2004 and 2012, before he was
extradited to America.

Now, since this is a book about my observations of British society.
I can safely say that polite words like 'thank you', 'please', and 'much
appreciated' definitely go a long way. So, you only have to imagine
how these already heavily burdened taxpayers felt when 'Abu Hamza'
refused to show gratitude, but continued to insult the country which
was giving him both shelter and status. He infamously replied to a
question he was once asked regarding the reason why he insulted
Britain although he had acquired its nationality and benefitted from
its assistance by saying:

"Because it is Bait Al Khala'[22] where I poop."

However, what is remarkable in the original story of Abu Hamza
was that he was not always an extremist. He arrived in Britain as a
student and he previously described it as a "heaven where one can

---

21 Source: The *Daily Express*, May 21st, 2014 – http://www.express.co.uk/news/uk/477268/
Abu-Hamza-s-family-allowed-to-stay-in-1-25-million-London-home-and-claim-33-800-
benefits

22 Bait Al Khala' is a term that means toilet or bathroom.

do what one pleases." He worked as a bouncer for a strip club before marrying a British woman who subsequently converted to Islam and is said to have convinced him to become religious and finish his studies in engineering in order to guarantee him and his family a secure future.

However, after divorcing his first wife, with whom he had one son, he married again and had seven children. At the time, his interest in political Islam became apparent. According to a profile published about him by BBC Arabic, he was influenced by the Iranian revolution in the early 1980s[23] and later decided to go to Afghanistan where he was injured. He came back to Britain for treatment. Two years later, Abu Hamza travelled again to Bosnia before coming back to Britain, rapidly rising as an Islamic leader and finally becoming the Imam of Finsbury Park Mosque in 1997.

Although all his horrific positions were expressed publicly, the authorities — for some reason — did not intervene to stop Abu Hamza's sermons until 2003. That year, the police raided the Mosque under the pretext of investigating a plan to produce toxic materials. The Mosque was closed and propaganda materials were confiscated. Despite the fact that Abu Hamza was not arrested during that operation, the Mosque's administration fired him. So, he continued to deliver his sermons every Friday in the street, outside of the mosque under the nose and protection of the British police.

In 2004, the United States issued an arrest warrant against him and asked Britain to extradite him there. However, this took place a bit late, while Abu Hamza was facing a local trial. His extradition did not happen until after Britain received guarantees from Washington that it would not torture or execute him, given the fact that Britain was a signatory of the European Convention on Human Rights, which prohibits the extradition of suspects to bodies or countries that might treat them inhumanly.

---

23 Source: the BBC Arabic website, April 14th, 2014 – http://www.bbc.com/arabic/world-news/2014/04/140414_abu_hamza_profile.

During his trial in America in 2014, Abu Hamza Al-Masri claimed, for the first time, that he was operating as a secret agent for British Domestic Intelligence (MI5) during his time at the Finsbury Park Mosque. He claimed that he had met with British security officials several times and that the arrangement that was in place required him to report any suspicious activities and to help with local interaction with the Muslim community.

Obviously, British security officials deny these claims, suggesting that Abu Hamza had exaggerated them. However, they did not deny that more than one meeting had been held with him. Critics of the British government claimed that the officials used the preacher when it suited them and abandoned him when he became too vocal about the Iraq War. What benefit could any government have gained from using such a heinous figure, or recruiting him as an agent? I have no idea.

No matter what the truth is, the reality of the situation is that the legacy of preachers of hate such as Abu Hamza, is a lesson that one can gain fame, money and a huge following by simply letting one's beard grow and making horrendous statements. Sadly, while the fictional Captain Hook's impact fades away as soon as the fairy tale is over, the damaged caused by the real life one — a.k.a. Abu Hamza — will remain and stain the image of British Muslims for a very long time.

CHAPTER VII

BELLE DE JOUR

Undoubtedly, London's red-coloured pay-phone booths (or 'telephone boxes' as they are more commonly known) are amongst the most famous – and exclusive – landmarks of the British capital. While these coin-operated calling cabins still retain their sentimental value, they have totally lost their practical significance following the proliferation of mobile phones in the mid-nineties.

Today, the few remaining red boxes tend to be deserted and in a deplorable condition due to lack of use. Now, they do say curiosity killed the cat, and I have to say I did come very close to killing myself out of disgust the first time I ventured into one of these booths back in 2004. Little did I know, at the time, that they are actually still widely in use, but only for particular kinds of calls…nature calls, to be specific! Apparently, after a long night of drinking, especially on cold winter evenings, these booths conveniently double for urinals. (This is especially true for those who are not bothered with washing their hands or leaving a stink behind.)

I say this with a lot of regret and sadness at what has become of this great invention – how civilised the British were to create these miraculous boxes! Inside a tiny, standing-room-only space, you are guaranteed not only your privacy as a caller, but also that you will not disturb anyone during the call. I can't escape this comparison every time I hear someone on their smartphone having a heated, or an intimate, discussion related to their work or personal life on a bus, or as they walk across the street.

Back in the early 2000s, these boxes were not yet completely dysfunctional. While their operators tried to make them more user-friendly and in tune with the time by allowing credit card payments and enabling Wi-Fi, they still served a particularly unique, albeit socially frowned-upon, function. Inside these cabins one typically found promotional flyers the size and shape of a postcard. These flyers advertised a wide range of sexual services offered by semi-naked (and sometimes fully naked) ladies and gentlemen, along with their aliases and phone numbers.

Skimming through these cards, a visitor would realize that London had something (or rather, someone) for every taste: from blondes to brunettes, from the size-zeros to the plus-sized and horizontal-ly-blessed body types, and age varieties ranging from the late teens to 'mature' grannies.

The cards also promoted different nationalities and ethnicities: from English Roses to Sensual Asians and from Eastern Europeans to Arabs and Africans. Of course, there were also more specific options, such as gay, lesbian and transgender offerings.

But wait just a moment – or should I say 'keep your shirt on' – before you jump to the conclusion that this means, by default, that prostitution is acceptable in British society. As is the case with most matters that require passing judgement, British perceptions and attitudes towards the 'oldest profession in history' constitute a bit of grey area. Naturally, many conservatives in society reject it. Others might simply sigh and shrug their shoulders in indifference when asked their opinions. Throughout, the Anglican Church warns against treating sex as a commodity. However, many liberals believe in the complete opposite and argue that people are free to use and profit from their body in the way they see fit.

Strictly speaking, there is no law in Britain that prohibits paying money for sex as long as it is not with minors, or with anyone coerced into the act. The only exception is Northern Ireland, which is the only country in the union that officially prohibits prostitution.[1]

In fact, His Majesty's Revenue and Customs (HMRC) actually imposes a tax on the revenues of prostitutes, stating clearly that "If the activities of a prostitute or any other person deriving income from prostitution are organised in such a way as to constitute a trade or profession, the profits are liable to Income Tax."[2]

As such, one could argue that, unlike in many other countries, especially Arab and Muslim ones, the only 'officers' British sex workers fear are not the police, but the tax collectors! Unlike a country like Iran, for example, where newspaper stories are often about members of the religious police raiding a brothel or lashing a sex worker, in the UK it is usually reports of tax evasions that make it to the front pages of the tabloids.

For example, back in 2012, an 'elite' sex worker was indeed imprisoned. This young lady's crime was not the actual act of selling her body for a hefty £1,000 per night, however. Rather, what she was charged and convicted for was evading taxes of more than £120,000! As for how she was caught, the young lady raised suspicions when she paid, cash and in advance, half the full price of a luxurious flat in the upscale Knightsbridge area. Since this particular lady came from a low-income family and was officially jobless and registered as a masters student in a London university, her ability to buy such a high-end property and the availability of

---

1 Northern Ireland prohibited prostitution on July 1, 2015.

2 Refer to the His Majesty's Revenues and Customs official site: https://www.gov.uk/hmrc-internal-manuals/business-income-manual/bim65001#:~:text=If%20the%20activities%20of%20a,v%20Aken%20%5B1990%5D%2063TC395.

so much cash in hand raised immediate red flags.

According to press reports, police found tens of thousands of pounds as well as expensive jewellery upon raiding her home. During her trial, the prosecution estimated that she had earned more than £300,000[3] between 2005 and 2007. In other words, she would have slept with 300 men – or a hundred men a year – at £1,000 per night, and this is not accounting for what the prosecution could not prove.

Putting aside tax evasion, some might be surprised – particularly given the phone booth cards story I started this chapter with – that while prostitution itself is not forbidden in Britain, the law actually prohibits its solicitation. Placing promotional photo cards inside phone boxes is therefore illegal, which is why they are often periodically removed. This is why brochures or websites that promote sexual services tend not to call acts or services by their actual names. This is also why some workers in the profession are known as 'escorts', and why some brothels are described as 'massage parlours'.

Agents booking escorts' appointments will always stress that what they are selling is the 'time' the client spends with their chosen companion. Agents typically go on to elaborate that 'anything that happens between the escort and the client during the paid-for-time is up to their discretion as two consenting adults.'

Okay, so by now you must be wondering: "How does this author know so much about this topic?" Before you let your imagination run wild, or make ethical (or should I say, unethical) assumptions about me, let me tell you that the answer is much more unexpected than you might think. Everything that I have mentioned and more – such as ways to circumvent laws and trick tax collectors – were publicly dramatised in a popular 2007 British television series called Secret Diary of a Call Girl. Well, they do say the best place to hide

---

3 Source: *Daily Telegraph*, 10th July 2012 –

http://www.telegraph.co.uk/finance/personalfinance/tax/9388075/1000-a-night-high-class-escort-jailed-over-120000-tzx-fraud.html is out there in full sight! What is even more fascinating about this television series is that its events are not fictitious, but rather based on real events published in two bestselling books in 2005 and 2006 that were written by a famous call-girl in Britain, nicknamed Belle de Jour.[4]

As you might expect, this series – starring the splendid singer/actress Billie Piper[5] in the role of Belle – triggered many mixed reactions. While some critics welcomed the series as being a remarkable work of dramatic art, others attacked it from a moral and social point of view as 'a glorification of prostitution' and 'portraying women as commodities'.

Now, whether or not HMRC officers watched this series or not, I don't know, but what is certain is that it doesn't paint them in a good light (considering that one of them actually sleeps with Belle in return for turning a blind eye on her tax returns!) It also sheds light on the eventful, and sometimes dangerous, secret world that is lived behind closed doors and on the bedsheets of London's five-star hotel rooms and affluent neighbourhoods.

Yet not everyone can afford to shell out £1,000 per night, or to rent a fancy flat in Mayfair or Chelsea. For many Londoners who opt to pay for sex, this can come at a much lower price, and in a much more common area.

Soho, in central London, is known to be the British capital's red light district, containing all sorts of 'massage parlours', erotic bars

---

4 Belle de Jour is the alias of a real London prostitute later found to be the social worker and American-British Author Dr. Brooke Magnanti. Magnanti says she worked as a prostitute between 2003 and 2004 for additional income to help her fund her doctorate studies that she completed two years later from the University of Sheffield, UK. Between 2005 and 2006, Belle de Jour wrote two books based on real facts between her and her clients: *The Intimate Adventures of a London Call Girl* and later *The Further Adventures of a London Call Girl*. The two titles formed the basis of the above-mentioned television series, which aired on the British channel ITV between 2007 and 2011.

5 Billie Piper was originally a singer and entered the UK pop charts at the age of just fifteen, the youngest female singer ever to enter the UK chart list. She has since appeared in countless TV, film and theatre shows to great acclaim.

and strip clubs. Soho is also full of sex shops that sell erotic films and magazines, seductive lingerie, as well as toys used by lovers during sex.

Obviously, I had never set foot inside a sex shop before arriving in London. This shouldn't be surprising to anyone when they consider that even talking publicly about sex was considered a taboo in many conservative Arab and Muslim societies.[6] On the other hand, I have to confess I also had an exaggerated image of London. Of course, this was no City of Angels and obviously, many 'indecent' things were allowed, especially in Soho; but this was not the jungle of absolute lust, infidelity and sexually transmitted infections that our teachers and clerics warned us of back home, when they talked – with contempt – of the 'sexual revolution' of the 1960s.[7]

In fact, many British people I met were not even interested in what goes on in Soho. As I mentioned, one of the first friends I made here was a fellow journalist called Damien. He came to visit me at my hotel during my first week in London. Since I was staying in Holborn at the time, he proposed to take me to a number of famous bookstores (such as Waterstones and Borders) which were still thriving and located at the time on Charing Cross, opposite Soho.

On the way, I saw a sex shop for the very first time. Right there and then, I froze. Not knowing what to do, I felt just like Aladdin:

---

6 Censorship bodies in most Arab countries block all pornographic websites, then censor their internal media. There is also not a single Arab country I know where sex toys or pornographic material are sold publicly.

7 The sexual revolution was a social movement that began in the early 1960s and continued until the beginning of the 1980s. This revolution challenged traditional values and customs in Western societies regarding extramarital sex, as well as the negative view of homosexuals. It was a revolution that was to result in the 'normalisation' of talk about sex and its handling in the media, and a whole range of changes: such as the loss of romantic relationships, the use of pills and condoms, premarital sex, nudity in public, same-sex marriage and, in time, the right to abortion. In addition, this revolution resulted in the lifting of the ban on previously banned industries such as the porn movie industry and the legalisation of brothels in several cities.

here I was, standing in front of the magical Cave of Wonders![8] Dare I enter? I must not touch, or be lured by anything, no matter how appealing it was. But the question in my mind was, do I even enter? Do I surrender to my curiosity, or do I ignore it?

I could not work out whether it was better for me to pretend that the store was not really of interest to me and just ask Damien subtly about it (with a plot to return to it alone if he said it was safe to go in) or embarrass myself and ask a man I had just met to walk into a sex shop with me!

Moments later, I found myself turning towards Damien, and saying innocently:

"Do you mind if we go in to take a quick look? I have never visited a place like this in my life."

Damien, without reacting or showing any emotion, just nodded and said: "Sure."

As we stepped in, my curiosity quickly turned into disappointment. I am not sure if this was due to religious or moral reasons, or simply because I felt the 'commoditisation' took away all the mystery. Just like a neighbourhood supermarket, the shop stacked erotic films, DVDs and intimate toys on shelves as if they were laundry detergent packs or cans of tuna fish. Customers casually shopped in the store carrying metal baskets, and picked up items as if they were buying fruit or vegetables! Some, for example, had no embarrassment about examining plastic toys in the shape of male genitalia, before returning them to the shelf or asking a friend (presumably their partner) what they thought of the size, colour and price. Above the items, promotional posters had slogans like "plastic has never been so fantastic" and "who needs boys when you've got toys?"

What was interesting about this experience was that it did not

---

8 The Walt Disney film *Aladdin* made much of the Cave of Wonders, which was based on the supposed caves where in Arabic mythology, King Solomon was supposed to have hidden his treasures. In the film, Aladdin is warned not to touch any of the treasures other than the famous lamp.

make you feel you were doing anything forbidden or awkward. In fact, the shop was so 'normal' that it even had a 'refunds and returns' policy. This meant customers had 14 working days to bring back their purchased items, return their money or swap an item for another product of the same value. Of course, given the nature of products being sold – such as the plastic male organ – one only has to imagine the conversation between the unsatisfied customer and the vendor. Most certainly, one also hopes that the shop wouldn't resell the same returned item to another customer![9]

What also surprised me was the absence of the concept of seduction in such a shop. In fact, there was nothing – perhaps except for some special offers and discounts on damaged or old merchandise – to attract the client or 'implicate' him in more 'vice'. There was no voluptuous woman in sexy clothes at the checkout. Instead, sitting behind the till was a skinny teenager with thick, messy hair and lots of acne (he was probably a student with a part-time job). In what is the absolute opposite of sexy (at least for me), this young man was chewing gum while reading a Spiderman comic book.

Every once in a while, customers would come to that teenager holding their metal shopping baskets carrying – so casually, as I mentioned earlier – products that they could not have realised were nearly impossible to obtain in many other countries except through the black market. Those who buy such products in our countries do it discretely for fear of punishment or scandal; the customers of this Soho store were coming out carrying bags with the name and logo of the shop!

But what surprised me the most is what I discovered about my British friend, Damien. As we walked out, I felt the need to explain myself, apologise for the detour and reiterate it was because this was my first time inside such a shop.

---

9 Trade regulations exclude returning some goods (such as underwear) that have been actually opened and used, in order to prevent the transmission of diseases and to ensure the ability to resell them!

"Not at all, it was my first time too," replied Damien without a hint of any emotion, and then moved onto another topic. This was a surreal situation for me, as before I arrived in the UK, many of my friends and family were worried that Westerners would corrupt my morals. Little did I, or anyone, know that it would be the other way around: in less than a week after my arrival, here I was corrupting them instead!

This small incident taught me the true meaning of our famous Arab saying, "Everything that is forbidden, is desirable." But what Damien, and my time in London, taught me, was that the opposite was also true: I never felt the urge to visit such a store again.

As for Damien, we remain very good friends twenty years later. I think, or rather hope, he has forgotten my very awkward request on the first day we met. Damien was always very understanding and incredibly cultivated; in the more than twenty years I have known him, I have never heard him once ridicule a culture or repeat a stereotype. On the contrary, he was and still is, fascinated with Arab culture and the Middle East in general.

The same, sadly, can't be said of many Westerners and their preconceived ideas of us Arabs. To many, we all fall into one of two categories: we are either rich and stupid, or extremists who are enemies of other cultures, Western values and co-existence.

In both cases, we are thought to be sexually insatiable. In the first case, there are many urban legends about the money that rich Arabs splash on lavish parties. These wild nights out are supposedly fuelled with excessive drug use and lots and lots of alcohol. This vision is, naturally, complemented by spending extravagantly on the most attractive and expensive call girls who come by the dozens.

In the second 'extremist' stereotype women are treated as second-class beings. They are found for the sole purpose of meeting a man's sexual needs. This image is, naturally, supported by the news of women being raped and taken as slaves by terrorist groups such as Daesh and Al-Qaeda.

Of course, while both stereotyped Arab categories do indeed exist, it is simply unfair to generalise. Seriously, how many terrorists or women-enslavers do you know? As for the crazy partying, well…isn't that exactly what Westerners say about wealthy Russians, Asians and Africans too? And what do young Brits get up to during their summer breaks in destinations such as Ibiza or Magaluf? They certainly don't go there to become nuns and priests!

I had to wrestle with a lot of ignorance and unpleasant stereotypes during my time in London. Partly, because I was driven and curious to learn and interact with others, but also because to many I was one of the few Saudis they had ever met in their lives.

On one occasion, about two years after I moved to London, I attended the birthday party of an female American journalist friend of mine who lived in London. Little did I know that I was going to be the only Arab in a flat full of Brits, Americans and Europeans. In such circumstances, I was used to being looked at like I was a plate of exotic fruit.

Halfway through the party, I met another female American journalist who happened to be visiting London. As soon as she got to know my ethnic background, she shocked me with a question which I felt was just incredibly inappropriate, especially as I hadn't known her before:

"Ah, you are an Arab. Y'all are really into your dominatrixes!"

I replied in exasperation: "Sorry, what?"

She explained that one of her friends back in the US was a dominatrix who had told her that many of her clients happened to be Arabs who were visiting America. She then asked me in a way that I was uncertain whether to interpret as genuinely curious or deliberately provoking:

"Is this because you oppress women in your countries, so when you come to the West you enjoy the opposite?"

Luckily, I had picked up a few useful British habits by that time. So, I responded in a cold, sarcastic way:

"Well, first I must say that you seem to have very interesting friends!" And then I added: "Secondly, I am sure your friend must have American clients too, so how does this fit into your fascinating theory?"

She did not seem to like my answer and told me that there was no need to be defensive, that she was only asking out of curiosity.

"Not at all," I replied. "I am curious too. Are you, and all Americans, like your former president, Bill Clinton?"

She replied: "I don't get it. What do you mean?"

"Oh! Don't you remember what Clinton did to his mistress, sorry, I mean his former intern, Monica Lewinsky? You see, based on your theory, I would assume you must also be into cigars, though not necessarily to smoke them!"[10]

At that point, that American journalist just walked away, murmuring angrily some words that I did not catch. Thankfully, I did not see her any more throughout the party. Of course, I wished that whole unnecessary conversation had not happened. At the same time, I won't lie to you and pretend that I was not a little bit satisfied with the outcome. Two years into my stay in London, I had finally started mastering the art of debating, and the skill of not allowing others to get under my skin.

Of course, there must be Arabs who see prostitutes, or even perhaps dominatrixes. But what bothers me is those who seem to like to suggest that we were the only ones doing it! Since prostitution is forbidden in all the Abrahamic religions (Judaism, Christianity, Islam) it is consequently viewed negatively across most societies so I do not see why some people act as if they are innocent and it is only Arabs who are guilty of the vice. One other argument I could have used with that American journalist was that of the Jeffery Epstein

---

10 In 1997, President Clinton conducted an affair inside the White House with a young intern called Monica Lewinsky. When the news broke, the story began to circulate that Ms Lewinsky had been offered a cigar in a particularly intimate manner.

scandal, although that didn't become public till years later.[11]

Of course, the British are far from being angels. According to 2009 statistics, one out of ten British men pays for sex. The number of prostitutes in the UK exceeds 61,000 and each one of these sex workers entertains an average of 5 clients a week.[12]

Again, these figures should not let us forget that – as mentioned before in this chapter – there are many in Britain who strictly oppose prostitution. In fact, there are many who actively campaign against any form of commoditisation of the female body, be it for religious, moral or political reasons.

It is also worth noting that decency is a fluid concept and society becomes more strict or more liberal depending on many factors. For instance, it is unthinkable in today's 'woke' climate that topless images of women should anymore be allowed in daily newspapers. However, for nearly five decades, British tabloids[13] were known for their 'page 3 girls': the tradition of publishing an image of a different topless woman on the third page on a daily basis.

---

11 Jeffery Epstein was an American financier who was first convicted in 2008 of having sex with underage girls. After a plea-bargaining deal, he served 13 months in jail before being released. He was re-arrested in 2019 on the charge of trafficking young girls for sex in Florida and was subsequently found dead in his cell in New York City a month after his arrest. The case brought into the open the possibility that many famous male figures might have been caught up in his activities but, at the time of writing, none has yet been formally accused.

12 Source: BBC Website, May,6 2015: https://www.bbc.co.uk/news/uk-northern-ireland-32539648

13 The name 'tabloid' is given to British daily newspapers that rely on sensationalism. These publications are characterised by looking for and revealing royal and celebrity scandals. They are also characterised by their smaller size and rectangular shape compared to the larger-page conventional and more respectable newspapers which are called 'broadsheets'.

The Sun newspaper,[14] owned by Rupert Murdoch, the global media mogul, pioneered this tradition in the British press in the 1970s and it was later followed by other tabloids. It is said that Murdoch was not happy with the idea at first. However, the editor-in-chief at that time persuaded him with figures. Thanks to these images, *The Sun's* sales rose from 1.5 million copies to 2.1 million copies in just one year.[15]

Thanks to such high circulation figures, it was inevitable that the page 3 girls would turn into celebrities with a huge fan base. They received serious money from lucrative sponsorship and collaboration offers (in a way, one can argue they were the ancestors of some modern day 'influencers' on social media).

Despite the popularity of this phenomenon among many readers, it had its critics in the United Kingdom. Many politicians, intellectuals and religious figures opposed it. Yet page 3 girls continued to appear in British tabloids – despite all the criticism – until 2015. On January 22nd of that year, Rupert Murdoch finally bowed to pressure and The Sun stopped publishing topless photos, bringing to a close a tradition that had run for 45 years.

Page 3 had been a launchpad for some of Britain's biggest celebrities

---

14 *The Sun* is a London-based daily tabloid that has long been the most widely distributed newspaper in the United Kingdom with two to three million copies distributed per day at one point. This newspaper remains one of the most influential newspapers to the point where many politicians are keen to gain its support and the support of its editor-in-chief during election campaigns. *The Sun* (normally a Conservative party affiliate) supported the Labour Party in 1997, allowing Prime Minister Tony Blair to win three consecutive terms. The paper stopped supporting the Labour Party in 2009, Blair's successor Gordon Brown lost and the Conservatives won under the leadership of David Cameron.

15 I wrote an article about this titled: "Page 3 beauties... The Sun's Not-So-Secret Weapon in the Circulation arena" in *Asharq Al-Awsat* newspaper, May 2nd, 2005.

http://archive.aawsat.com/details.asp?issueno=9532&article=301886.2005

and pop stars. Among them were famous singers Samantha Fox[16] and former Spice Girls member Geri Halliwell.[17] One could argue that they both owe it to The Sun for 'revealing their talents' at an early stage of their careers.

But just because appearing topless brought fame and fortune to some of Britain's beauties, one shouldn't assume it has the same effect in other countries. In fact, quite the contrary…and no, I am not talking about Afghanistan, Iran or the Vatican. I am talking about the United States of America. Many do not realise the great difference between American and British cultures regarding decency and what is allowed in the media. Some (and I was among them) mistakenly believed that the American media was more liberal on the subject of nudity.

All I can say to those who think this is that they have to remember that during the era of page 3 girls, The Sun used to be sold perfectly normally in British grocery shops. Minors could buy a copy just as they would buy crisps, soft drinks or chocolate, whereas any media material involving similar nudity would be subject to strict procedures in the United States. Over there, it is strictly forbidden to sell or display similar material to those under the age of 18.

What happened to the famous US singer Janet Jackson during her performance at the halftime show at the 2004 American Football

---

16 Samantha Fox was an international award-winning English singer, born in 1966. She had great musical success in the 1980s. Fox began her career in the world of fame by showing her nude photos in *The Sun* in 1983 when she was 16 years' old and lasted four years, during which she achieved tremendous fame until she began her musical career in 1986.

17 Geri Halliwell was a member of the British band Spice Girls, which became famous in the 1990s. She sold more than 80 million records during her career with the band. Halliwell also made a remarkable move as a solo singer after breaking up with the team. As with Samantha Fox, Geri also began her career in the world of fame by topless modelling for *The Sun* when she was 19 years' old.

Super Bowl,[18] is a striking paradox in this context if compared to the situation in Britain. While performing a song with fellow US singer Justin Timberlake, her blouse fell and part of her chest appeared for about half a second before the situation was remedied. But that half of a second was enough to create an uproar in America, especially since millions were watching the show live on television.

Despite Janet's and the organisers' apology, and the assertion that it was an inadvertent mistake, it did not prevent broadcaster CBS being fined $550,000. (This also caused trials, and legal cases, which lasted until 2012 and ended with the acceptance of the network's appeal and the cancellation of the fine.)

Many of my English friends ridiculed the case. Commenting on the incident, one of them said to me:

"Americans really need to relax. It's just a nipple! They would not have minded their children watching an action film, or playing a video game, where someone literally smashes another person's skull, but perish the thought, all hell would break lose if they saw a woman take off her top!"

How would the Janet Jackson incident have played in Arab societies if she was performing in Cairo, Riyadh or Abu Dhabi? Not well, obviously!

Will our attitudes towards such topics become more relaxed like the UK or uptight like the US? I don't know, but you can depend on me to keep you 'abreast' of the situation!

---

18 Super Bowl is the name given to the final game of the US National Football League (NFL). This game was first held in 1967. Since then, it is held on the last Sunday of January or the first Sunday of February each year. The match is a television event with distinction with the final typically enjoying an audience of over a hundred million viewers. Advertisers pay huge sums of money on Super Bowl television commercials. One of the most popular ads displayed at this event was Apple's Macintosh computer ad in 1984.

Chapter VIII

ROMEO AND JULIET

Of all the stereotypes presented of us, the Arabs, the one that holds the most truth is how fiery and emotional we get when it comes to love (or hate). It's true, we become very expressive and highly animated with our emotions. Countless are the times when British passers-by thought I was having a heated argument with an Arab friend, when the truth was, I was just telling them a funny joke in our mother tongue!

Of course, we think the complete opposite of the Brits. To us, most of you are completely cold and incapable of expressing feelings beyond saying a word or two, even when you are madly in love. Perhaps the best depiction of this perception is the one brilliantly portrayed by British-Iranian comedian, Omid Djalili, in one of his most famous sketches. Djalili describes how an Iranian man (with whom we Arabs have a lot in common, despite neither of us acknowledging this fact) expresses his feelings to his English girlfriend.

He says to her:

"I love you so much! I love you so much, I'm going to...I'm going

to...cut off my arm! I'm going to write you a poem in my own blood!"
Then he imitates taking out a knife and slashing at his arm, scrawling
imaginary words in the imaginary blood, then shouting passionately:
"Read it! Read it!"

The young Englishwoman reacts to this extraordinary outburst of
passion with: "Oh, thanks," as she appears to wander off, poem in
hand.[1]

Of course, this sketch maybe a bit exaggerated, but it is not very
far from an actual story that one of my Arab colleagues told me.
Abdul Latif is a Palestinian who was married to an Englishwoman for
a while, before divorcing for reasons that are very close to the ones in
Djalili's performance. Abdul Latif told me one day:

"Can you believe that my ex-wife — in the middle of an intense
and heated argument about the future of our relationship — decided
to suddenly stop talking and asked me to postpone the discussion,
because now it was her reading time?" He elaborated: "What
frustrated me was that while I was left with my blood boiling and
questions unanswered, she had completely switched off in the other
room, taken out a pencil and started underlining sentences that she
wanted to discuss in her book club the next day."

Of course, there are those who do not see any coldness or
indifference in such behaviour at all. Some may even look at it as a
form of wisdom. Someone suggested that Abdul Latif's wife's reaction
was correct, because it allowed both parties to calm down and reflect
before continuing the discussion on another day.

Yet the question remains: how, why, and when did the reputation
of the British go from passionate lovebirds to being so stone-cold,
to the point where they are the top choice for the roles of villains in

---

1 You can view Omid's sketch on YouTube: https://www.youtube.com/watch?v=-1wchcTak9Q

Hollywood films?[2] Lest you forget, we are talking about the same people and culture that gave us Shakespeare's Romeo and Juliet, one of the most romantic stories ever written.[3]

One suggestion, made by the historian Claire Langhamer, is that an 'emotional revolution' took place in England following the First World War, with more people marrying at a younger age. By the middle of the century, romantic love in Britain had become inextricably attached to sexual satisfaction; by the end of the century, it was located at the heart of modern marriage. As love achieved this new position in the making and success of marriage, it also became more difficult to sustain.[4]

Like most stereotypes, it is an exaggeration and inaccurate to describe the British as being "cold." Personally, I think they are very affectionate, but the difference lies in the way they express — or rather don't express — their feelings, compared to us Arabs. This is as true when it comes to love as it is when it comes to grieving. In both cases, it is very un-British to expose your emotions to others, whether it is overwhelming joy or suddenly bursting into tears — you will rarely see it in public.

Furthermore, I think modern Brits believe that actions speak louder than words. Indeed, while a British woman (or man) might feel awkward

---

2 There are many examples of this phenomenon, and there is almost unanimity that Hollywood prefers to give the roles of villains to British actors, and that they excel in these roles. The most famous examples of this are the performances of actors such as Anthony Hopkins as Hannibal, Christopher Lee as Dracula, Billie Whitelaw as Damien in *The Omen*, and even the voice of the evil lion Scar in the animated movie *The Lion King* — produced by Disney in 1994 — was performed by British actor Jeremy Irons (while all the voices of the good characters, such as the lions Simba and Mufasa, were performed by American actors). See this article in the *Daily Telegraph*: https://www.telegraph.co.uk/news/2017/01/22/british-accents-perfect-film-villains-makes-appear-less-trustworthy/

3 *Romeo and Juliet* was one of Shakespeare's earlier plays, written in the 1590s. Set in the Italian city of Verona, it depicts a fierce rivalry between two families, the Capulets and the Montagues. The two star-crossed lovers, Juliet Capulet and Romeo Montague, are caught up in the crossfire of the feud.

4 Claire Langhamer's book, The English in Love: The Intimate Story of an Emotional Revolution, is reviewed in *Reviews In History* here: https://reviews.history.ac.uk/review/1539

or embarrassed when confronted with a barrage of compliments, a kind gesture can go a long way. I once met an English marriage lawyer who was a beautiful young blonde lady from a well-off family and worked in a top law firm in Central London. She mentioned she was looking forward to her approaching wedding. As for the groom, he was a young stage actor who — unlike his fiancée — had not yet been successful in his field. He was just starting to make his way in the industry, landing minor roles here and there. They had dated for a few years and when the young actor had finally proposed to his fiancée and been accepted, he surprised her by announcing that he had spent all his savings (a few thousand pounds) on a romantic trip to the Caribbean. Upon hearing the story, his lawyer fiancée's father — who was a wealthy businessman — gifted his daughter and her future husband one of the houses he owned, as a token of his appreciation of how happy the young actor made his beloved daughter.

As you can imagine, this story is so romantic that every time I tell it to my British friends, their immediate reaction is almost always a sweet smile followed by a heartfelt "Awww!"

Ironically, whenever I tell the same story to some of my (mostly male) Arab friends, their reaction is generally sarcastic, such as:

"Attaboy! He got a pretty girl and house for life, for a few thousand quid!"

However, most Arab women I know would not say anything of the sort. Rather, they would just nervously smile and simply say "Oh, how sweet." Asked if they would be happy to marry an amateur actor (or even a professional one), most of them would politely shake their heads, citing the social pressure which dictates that they should go with someone better off who works in a 'serious' industry.

As for the English lawyer herself, I once asked her what her family or friends thought of her decision to marry the actor. Did anyone ever look down or persuade her to change her mind, because she was from a more well-off family and had a better paying job? Dumbfounded, she answered:

"Why should they even have a say on this matter? The only thing that should matter to them is whether I am happy with him or not."

This is where one has to wonder: are we Arabs really more romantic that the British? The answer naturally depends on who you ask, and how you define falling in love. To really understand what I mean, you should compare the English lawyer's love story to a personal story which happened between me and an attractive single Syrian lady I once met in London.

She was blonde (her hair's natural colour was brown, but she dyed it blonde), with light soft skin and a fine physique. She dressed elegantly but always in a way that drew everyone's attention, with a combination of skinny jeans and high heels. She was also keen on showing off her collection of designer bags which only added to her elegance from afar.

I was eager to meet this lady since she was the centre of attention of both my male and female Arab friends and I had consequently heard much about her. She was the dream girl to many of my single guy friends, and the trendsetter to many of my female friends who always sought to copy her look and style.

So I was thrilled when a group of friends tried to set the two of us up, given that I was also single at the time. One weekend I was invited to meet her, alongside my friends, at Café Nero by High Street Kensington Station. As much as I would love to tell you that she got me at "Hello!" it was actually the complete opposite. In fact, I don't think she even greeted me — what I do recall her saying when she first met me was:

"What does your father do for a living?"

This was followed by a series of 'qualifying questions' that seemed odd (at least to me) to ask someone you have just met. Her inquiry went as far as what type of car I drove when I went back home. The conversation did not go very much further when I told her that my father (may God rest his soul) had actually passed away, and that I did not drive.[5] I didn't feel comfortable with her line of questioning, or the whole vibe, which felt more like a cross-examination than a casual get-together. So, I finished my coffee and excused myself after wishing her, and everyone at the table, a good evening.

Less than three months after that meeting, I received — along with a group of friends — a surprise invitation to attend her wedding at a luxury hotel in London. Although we later learnt that the newlyweds had only known each other for a few weeks prior to their nuptials, they danced the night away and seemed extremely happy and in love...as if they had been together for years.

Could this have been love at first sight, or was it a marriage of convenience? I don't know. However, what I do know is that the groom was a well-known and wealthy Arab businessman, a good twenty years older than the bride. As such, one could safely assume that at least she did not have to ask him what his father did for a living on their first encounter.

But let us get back to those 'cold' Brits, shall we? Let us assume that they, as a people, have been socially conditioned to control their emotions to the maximum. Still, there must be a boiling point, right? And as such, the question that I tried hard to answer was: when do Brits lose their cool?

Surely, I assumed, cheating on your partner must be on top of the list. Yet even something like that triggered different reactions, and not necessarily aggressive ones.

For example, take what happened once with my personal trainer, Dan. During the first year of working out with him, he told me that he was in love with Claire, his childhood neighbour. I felt bad for him when he told me that he was unable to profess his interest in her, as she was in a relationship with another man.

According to Dan, Claire's boyfriend — who was tall and muscular

---

5 I never needed to drive at that point in my life, as I had lived in a boarding school during my high school years in Jordan, within walking distance of my university in Lebanon and I relied on public transport in London which was a lot more convenient and economical.

— worked as a bouncer in one of London's most famous nightclubs. Although Claire was a sweet girl who excelled academically and was loved by all her friends, this thug boyfriend of hers was, according to Dan, abusive and rude. He even had the audacity to go out in public with other girls every now and then, just to tease her!

So, I was very pleased when Claire finally decided to leave this bouncer and give Dan the chance I thought he deserved. Dan was polite and handsome despite his short stature, and more importantly, he was truly in love with her. He was also a true gentleman who, unlike many other athletes, was not obsessed with his body, nor was he arrogant because of his agility and muscular physique. On the contrary, he was kind to the point where he would volunteer to train orphans to play football once a week.

After a year of dating, Dan and Claire's relationship came to an end. He found out on Valentine's Day that she still had feelings for her ex-boyfriend and that she was secretly seeing the thug behind his back! The news hit me like a like a ton of bricks during one of our training sessions, but my true shock came upon hearing Dan's reaction when I asked him what he was going to do about the situation.

He told me: "We will end our relationship after Easter."

"What? Why after Easter?" I asked, surprised.

"Because a few months back we booked a holiday away together and cancelling now would be too costly," he said, calmly. "So she and I decided to go enjoy Easter together and then stop seeing each other once we get back."

I couldn't believe what I had heard. I started picturing what would have happened if the same situation occurred with an Arab couple. Well, the 'starter' would have been an exchange of insults, followed by a round of complaining to each other's parents and best friends in a bid to shame the other party. The 'main dish' would have been a heated argument, most probably in public, followed by a 'dessert' of what we call in Arabic 'exposing each other's dirty laundry'.[6]

Now, while reactions would of course vary between one Arab couple and another, the only thing which I could tell you in certainty is that this pre-booked holiday, no matter the cost, would have been cancelled (either by choice, or due to a restraining order!).

But then again, I also see it from Dan's point of view. I mean, if the separation is inevitable, why waste time on drama and bickering, right? Also, the way he sees it is, if he doesn't go on the holiday he already paid half the price for, it would only mean that Claire's 'thug' boyfriend would take his place.

However, if you were to ask me if I would I go on holiday with someone who cheated on me? Absolutely not. Still, I have to admire that Dan, despite what Claire did to him, never said a nasty word about her behind her back for the total of five years that I trained with him.

Not everyone in Britain is so calm or gentle. The tabloids are full of outrageous stories about make-ups and break-ups. Some of these stories are actually very entertaining. Once, a woman in Sheffield reportedly rented a giant billboard on her husband's commute to work, on which she wrote:

"To my cheating husband Paul, you deserve each other. When you come home I won't be there. Enjoy your drive to work."[7]

In another story of revenge, a man dumped a truckload of horse manure on his wife's convertible in Lincolnshire, a county on the east of Britain. Why? He found out that his wife was secretly looking for a lover on a dating website. The discovery happened after the wife accidentally left her profile page open on the couple's shared computer.

It seems that the husband lost his temper when he read that his

---

6 A phrase used in Britain as well as in Arabic countries, this means revealing embarrassing secrets or gossiping about personal details inappropriately in public.

7 Source: The Guardian, 2015: https://www.theguardian.com/uk-news/2015/sep/23/enjoy-your-drive-to-work-sheffield-woman-takes-revenge-on-cheating-husband

wife described him as a 'crazy idiot'. She also wrote that she no longer loved him, and that her only two loves were her convertible and her horse. Feeling insulted, the man plotted what can describe as a very British 'Honour Crime'[8] that would get back at his wife, her car, and her horse at the same time. The story got a huge amount of publicity at the time but was later claimed to be a PR stunt to promote that dating site.

By now, you may be wondering whether I will get into my personal juicy bits and tell you about my romantic life, dating attempts and break-ups. I hate to disappoint, but one must be mindful of a golden rule in British etiquette which stipulates that 'a gentleman never tells'. Therefore, I find myself bound to refrain from mentioning any names or intimate details about my relationships. Besides, I know that you too — my respected readers — do not intend to ask me about the subject at all, in conformity with another rule: a gentleman never asks!

But before you let your imagination run wild, thinking I have much to hide or that I was a consummate womaniser, allow me to ease your minds by confessing upfront that my failed attempts exceed by far my successes (by the way, you should know that any man who claims otherwise is just an elaborate liar!)

The reason for my failed relationships depends — of course — on who is telling the story. In general, I have come to learn, although too late, that as a man, you are either right...or in a relationship! I have also come to learn, too late as well, the value of the wise words of the

---

8 What Arabs describe as 'Honour Crimes' are very serious, involving physical attacks and murder following on from accusations of adultery. These typically involve a woman's wider tribe or direct family. They are common in countries such as Jordan, although such 'honour crimes' are discouraged and officially illegal.

late Irish writer Oscar Wilde,[9] who said, "Women are meant to be loved, not understood."

Like the Iranian man whom Omid Djalili described in his comedy routine mentioned earlier in this chapter, I found out after a while that too much passion had an adverse impact, as opposed to an endearing one, particularly with British ladies. Now, while it was not my fault all the time, I have to confess that I made my fair share of mistakes. The only reason I do not list them all is that I would need an entire encyclopedia, not just a chapter in a book, to capture them.

Nevertheless, you did pay to be entertained by this book, so here you go. I once went out to dinner with an Italian beauty (she was actually a model, with long curly black hair, hazel eyes and a sweet smile). To impress her, I took her out to a famous Italian restaurant called Signor Sassi in upscale Knightsbridge.

As soon as we were seated, I began pretending to be an expert on everything Italian. I used terms like buona sera (good evening) and grazie (thank you) when talking to the Italian waiter. I then began to praise the excellent food in this particular restaurant, telling her that it was the closest she could get to her homeland's authentic dishes.

However, my exaggerations started to unravel quickly, as I made a fatal mistake once my lobster spaghetti arrived. I cannot describe the extent of the shock painted on the faces of both the lady and the waiter when I ordered some grated Parmesan cheese to sprinkle over the pasta. The waiter cringed and did not know what to say. Meanwhile, my date's face turned red as she said in exasperation,

---

9 Oscar Wilde (1854-1900): famous Irish playwright, poet, journalist and novelist. He rose to fame through his popular plays in London, in the 1890s. Wilde is known for his scathing comments and wisdom. Among his most famous works translated into Arabic are: *The Picture of Dorian Gray* (translated by Louis Awad), *The Canterville Ghost* (translated by Louis Awad), *A Woman of No Importance* (Translated by Michel Abdel Ahad) and *An Ideal Husband* (translated by Fawzi Semaan).

"Faisal, you never put cheese on seafood!"[10]

Needless to say, that was the 'Last Supper' with that young lady. Not just because of my 'cheesiness', but because the night ended with the waiter getting her phone number (they turned out to be from same part of Italy, and judging by the exciting conversation which took place in their language, I wouldn't be surprised if they are happily married today) while the only number I ended up with was the figure on the bill.

Nevertheless, the situation was a lesson for me, not only about the do's and don'ts of Italian dining, but also when it comes to the importance of being authentic and not pretending to be someone I am not. Most importantly, I learnt that it is better to take a lady out — if she is Italian, for instance — to an Arab restaurant and not one she is familiar with.

Since the incident at Signor Sassi, I opted to conduct my conquests at the nearby Maroush instead. This Lebanese restaurant on Beauchamp Place (also in Knightsbridge) has been witness to many of my successes in this regard. At that place, amongst my kith and kin, I was able to flaunt my knowledge of culture and history. Along with every dish was an opportunity to brag about the depth of Arab civilisation, compared to the British, when it comes to food. (I used sometimes even to go so far as to explain the difference between the Egyptian, Lebanese and Palestinian ways of preparing falafel, for example.)

You can imagine how the tables were turned in Maroush, compared to what happened to me in Senior Sassi, when I had to scold (very gently, of course) a British date I once took to dinner, explaining to her that baklava cannot be dipped in hummus!

As for relationships and dating among Arabs in London, there is no doubt that they can be complicated. There is no escape from that

---

10 Italians take their food very seriously. And there are restaurants that categorically refuse, for example, to serve ketchup with pizza because it 'ruins' its original taste. (and no, I do not put ketchup on my pizza!).

uncomfortable feeling that some of us get when we go out with our fellow compatriots abroad. This is probably due to a range of factors such as our parents' mutual acquaintances or concern about one's reputation in one's homeland. For example, a young Arab man in the West is accused of wanting to 'have fun' before settling down and want to 'experience everything' with a Western girl, after which he will go on to marry a young woman from a small village in his country who, as the Arabic saying goes, "has never been kissed on the mouth by anyone apart from her mother."

While this stereotype certainly fits some young Arab men, I can assure you that there are Arab women who do not fall short on this front as well. I once met a beautiful young British woman of Egyptian origin who worked in the field of public relations. Her skin was tanned, she had silky black hair, long legs and beautiful black eyes like Cleopatra.

However, she shocked me, from the moment we met, by her alarming contradictions. While she was born in London, she seemed to dislike the culture of this country and Western culture in general, describing the English as "a group of filthy drunks."

I asked her the first time we met if she was engaged or seeing someone. She jolted me by replying angrily:

"Do you consider this generation of boys to be real men? Where are the likes of our great Islamic leaders, such as Khalid ibn al-Walid and Omar ibn al-Khattab?"[11]

I was not sure if she really meant what she was saying, or if she was assuming that such expressions would appeal to me, since I came from a Muslim country. She often asked me if I prayed and fasted and was also careful not to be seen alone with me, making one of her friends tag along at all times as a chaperone.

---

11 Khalid ibn al-Walid was a famous seventh-century Arab warrior who led Arab forces in battles against Arabian tribes and in Sassanid Iraq and who also led his troops to victory against Byzantine Syria. Omar ibn al-Khattab was the second Caliph to succeed Prophet Mohammed and he was known to be the firmest, but fairest of the early Islamic Caliphs.

Frankly, all of this did not bother me, but I thought that there was some exaggeration in her conservative behaviour, given the time and place in which we lived. She was not veiled; on the contrary, she used to party a lot and go out to nightclubs (although she was never seen drinking alcohol, or with a young man by herself). I asked her, gently, about these contradictions, especially since her field of work required her to mingle and, sometimes, to stay up late at events with clients and journalists. She replied that she made it clear to everyone from the beginning that she was looking for a committed Muslim husband and a true Arab, who would make her a housewife! She claimed to prefer men from the Gulf, whom she described as still true to those values.

On one occasion, I was very moved when she showed me a picture of her grey-haired father, whose face was lit with kindness. She explained that her father — who she told me had passed away years ago — had asked her to maintain a good reputation and reminded her that "a girl's honour is like a matchstick."[12]

Since I was not as much in a rush to get married as she was, and since she would only see me if I committed to a 'serious' relationship, she eventually lost interest in me and we haven't seen each other since. The last thing I expected was to discover, several years later, that this same woman had been in a relationship with an English journalist (a Christian, I must add for context) whom I got to meet by coincidence. He decided to tell me that he had once dated an Egyptian woman, something he mentioned only because I was an Arab, and, as we became closer, he later showed me photos of him and this ex-girlfriend. To my shock, the photos that he showed me were of the same young woman who was talking to me about Khalid ibn al-Walid and Omar ibn al-Khattab. Judging by the date of the photos, they were from the same period in which I was going out with her! What I also discovered was that he had been dating her in

---

12 This is an old Arabic saying, which means that, once a match has been lit, it – like a woman's "honour" – can never be lit again.

secret, at her request: she had told him that her father — I no longer knew whether he really was dead — would kill her if he knew she was seeing an Englishman. According to the fellow journalist, their secret relationship did not end until the woman married an Arab man "in compliance with her father's pressures."

Despite his grief over the end of their relationship, the English journalist seemed confident that his girlfriend would sooner or later find her way back to him. He told me with a bit of shyness, that the woman had told him that she "could not stand abstruse Arabs, who beat their wives."

Of course, I remained silent and never — until this day — revealed that I knew her, or that she was telling me the exact opposite about the English. After all...a gentleman never tells!

CHAPTER IX

MIND YOUR LANGUAGE

As you might have guessed by now, I was determined to make the most of my stay in London. This is why I took a decision in 2006 to continue my higher education – I was living in a country renowned for its academic institutions. As I needed to fund myself, I would have to continue working, so I began looking for a part-time Masters course that wouldn't impact my work hours or commitments.

An important aspect that I needed to take into account was the location of the university's campus. This made me narrow my options down and only focus on the universities located in Central London, to ensure that I would be able to make it to my lectures on time.

After that, I had to look for a field of study that complemented my career ambitions. In the end, it was down to three options: I could study Media and Communications at the London School of Economics (LSE), which was just a few minutes walking distance from where I worked in Holborn; I could join the Department of Journalism at London's City University; or the third option was to enrol in the Marketing Communications Masters Programme at

Westminster University's Business School.

Westminster had several campuses, but the Business School in particular was located in central London. Specifically, it was on Baker Street, facing the Madame Tussauds wax museum and the statue of the most famous fictional British detective, Sherlock Holmes.[1]

Of course, each university had its own system and requirements. City's Department of Journalism, which was the first one to accept me, focussed more on the personal interview. What helped me get into City was the fact that it was keen to attract professional journalists from different backgrounds. The fact that I was working at the *Ashaq Al-Awsat* newspaper, a leading Arab daily, definitely supported my application.

As for LSE, the application process was more complex, and it was the only institution to require a fee (£50) to be paid in order to review the application. To be honest, after reviewing the acceptance criteria, I felt for a moment as though I was applying for a job at a British private members club in Mayfair rather than at an academic institution. It felt like the focus was more on peripheral matters such as the personal letter that we had to annex and send to the admissions office with our application. In it, we had to state the reasons why we wanted to study. I considered this to be ridiculous. After all, it is pretty obvious why people undergo higher education: to improve your career prospects. In the unlikely situation of someone secretly plotting to use the degree to take over the world, for instance, I doubt he or she would actually declare that on the form.

Securing an acceptance at the University of Westminster wasn't necessarily easier, but the steps were much more straightforward. The

---

1 Sherlock Holmes is a fictional homicide detective created by the British novelist, Sir Arthur Conan Doyle. Holmes was known, through Doyle's short novels and stories, for his unique observation skills, forensic science skills and analytical thinking. Since Doyle specified that Holmes lived in apartment 221B on Baker Street, a museum was set up there for the lovers of this character. There is also an iconic statue of Holmes, who is famous for his traditional deerstalker hat and curved smoking pipe, standing outside Baker Street Station in central London.

only thing I tried to object to, but then ended up doing anyway, was taking the English language exam known as IELTS.[2] I still had to take this basic-level exam despite my specifying in my application that I spoke English fluently and had attended a Jordanian boarding school that followed the British IGCSE[3] system, as well as graduated from an American university in Lebanon. Alas, it was the whole 'computer says no' response from Little Britain all over again, so it was clear to me that arguing would not get me anywhere.

Therefore, I went to take the exam. Naturally, I finished the written part quickly. By the time I went into the oral exam, the examiner — as expected — was surprised at my ability to speak English, and asked me why I was even taking the test. I explained that after nearly three years living in London, I had learned not to wrestle with the system, and then I opted to crack a joke. I explained that, after some calculation, I figured out that it would be cheaper and quicker just to take the IELTS exam than arguing with the Admissions Officer or writing an objection letter.

"Do you know what is funny? My conversation with the Admissions Officer who was asking how she could verify that I could speak English...was in English!" I told the examiner.

I added that the whole incident reminded of that Mind Your Language episode where an Arab sheikh walks into the Ms Courtney's (the Principal's) office and enquires about evening classes. She asks him why he wants to enrol given that his English is impeccable.

"Thank you, it is comforting to know my years at Oxford were not wasted," says the sheikh. "I would like my personal chauffeur to join your class."

---

2 Established in 1989, the International English Language Testing System (IELTS) is an international standardised test assessing the English language proficiency of non-native speakers. Jointly managed by the British Council, IDP: IELTS Australia and Cambridge Assessment English, it has gathered widespread recognition over the years.

3 The International General Certificate of Secondary Education (IGCSE) is an English language secondary qualification which sits alongside the British GCSE and as such is recognised in Britain as being equivalent.

Ms Courtney then asks where the Sheikh's chauffeur is from and is surprised, when he walks into the office, to find he is from Glasgow.

"He's Scottish?" asks Ms Courtney. "But why do you want us to teach him English?"

"Because I can't understand a word he says!" replies the sheikh.

The examiner burst out laughing and responded by saying:

"You are not just a wise person, Faisal…you are a funny man too!"

He asked me how I knew Mind Your Language. I explained that it was a very popular show on Saudi Arabian television Channel 2 in the 1980s.[4]

Eventually, I was accepted by both 'City' and 'Westminster', while LSE rejected my application. I guess they might have not liked my "reason for wanting to study" there. And in case you were wondering: no, I didn't say that my reason was to take over the world! Although, one has to wonder what Saif al-Islam Gaddafi, son of the late Libyan dictator Muammar Gaddafi, handwritten (or had had written for him) for his controversial application to be accepted at this prestigious London institution.[5]

Nevertheless, I still had two excellent offers to choose from. The choice was difficult but it was the honest advice I received from Professor Adrian Monck, the Head of Journalism at City University at the time, that helped make up my mind. He told me that I was welcome at his school, but that City University's course already covered my field of work. Adrian thought I had a lot of experience

---

4 *Mind Your Language* was a British comedy which first appeared on ITV in 1977. The comedy revolved around the interaction of a cast of people from different countries and different backgrounds all gathered together in a classroom to learn English. It is not shown on British TV any more, as its approach to racial stereotyping has fallen foul of contemporary attitudes. The commissioner, Michael Grade, now says he thinks it should never have been on TV.

5 In 2008, Saif Gaddafi was awarded a PhD from the Department of Philosophy at LSE for a dissertation entitled *The Role of Civil Society in the Democratisation of Global Governance Institutions*. Very soon after the award, a charity run by Saif offered to give LSE £1.5m over a five-year period. It has been alleged by several parties that the dissertation was ghostwritten by someone else.

and knowledge, and that rather than studying there he suggested I take a job teaching in a special programme the university was undergoing in Bahrain.

Adrian's advice — which ended up being crucial for my career — was to go and learn how to manage, as opposed to continue being managed. At this stage, however, I considered that studying for a Masters in Marketing Communications at Westminster University's Business School would add a new dimension to my professional life, so I chose to go there. The course was multi-dimensional, including lectures on marketing campaigns management, consumer psychology, reputation management and public relations.

I have to confess, I had a slightly outdated idea about studying in the UK and how formal it was. But this outdated perception was very quickly dismissed after just a few lectures. On my first day at university, I wanted to ask my consumer psychology lecturer a question. His name was Frank Auton. So, I raised my hand and called him "Sir". I suddenly felt the heads of all my colleagues in the lecture hall turn towards me with astonishment. Frank turned to me, smiled a little and adjusted his glasses before patting me on the shoulder, saying:

"There is no need for that. Call me Frank!"

Naturally, the fact that this was a postgraduate degree made a difference in the nature of the relationship, as the students in this case – by default – were not minors or teenagers but young professionals. But also, as I got to know the lecturers, I discovered they were genuinely nice, humble people. I felt that they were as eager to learn from me as I was from them.

There was a sharp contrast between this attitude and that of some teachers I had met throughout my childhood in Saudi Arabia, Jordan and Lebanon. For example, I still specifically remember the Egyptian science teacher who taught me in second grade of middle school in Jeddah. He used to enter the class with a grim face and, as soon as he crossed the doorstep, he would order all the students to stand up out of respect for him, saying: "All rise!" We would remain standing until he ordered us to sit down.

During his first class that school year, I did not notice that he had arrived as I was looking inside my bag for my books. I remained seated with my backpack on my lap and my head inside of it. He came into class, ordered us to stand up, then strode over and knocked my backpack, yelling at me:

"Throw away the garbage you have in your hands and stand up when I order you to do so! Do you understand, you piece of garbage?"

I also remember a third-grade Syrian mathematics teacher who choked me once. Perhaps that is why, even today, I still hate maths!

I regret not reporting these incidents to my parents or to the school administration at the time. But also, I have to say that this was not the norm. There were distinguished teachers that I still remember and respect with plenty of admiration.

The situation was completely different in Britain, as laws here prohibit beating, insulting and personally targeting any student. In addition, it seems that the main problem in most schools is the teachers complaining about being abused by the students…not the other way round!

For example, according to a report published by the National Association of Schoolmasters Union of Women Teachers (NASUWT) in 2015, eight out of every ten teachers in Britain had suffered verbal abuse. The same report also pointed out that 23 percent of the teachers had also complained about receiving threats, while seven per cent of them said that they had actually been subjected to physical assault at the hands of students![6]

Of course, this is what used to take place in elementary, middle and high school; the dynamics were quite different for higher education, as I mentioned before. We enjoyed a peer-to-peer relationship

---

6 Source: The *Daily Telegraph*, April 4th, 2015 – https://www.telegraph.co.uk/education/educationnews/11513868/Schools-failing-to-expel-students-who-bully-teachers-as-verbal-abuse-in-the-classroom-soars-by-a-third.html

with most lecturers. In fact, we were regularly asked to assess the lecturers at the end of each term. In addition, there was an elected Student Council, which represented the interests and opinions of the students through elected representatives who had the right to challenge many of the university's decisions, address the students' issues and problems, demand their resolution, organise their needs and speak to the press if necessary.

I had never experienced going through an election before so I was keen to go through the experience and feel what it means to be an elected official. However, before you get carried away and imagine that I fought battles that will be told in history books, I must clarify that the most significant of the demands I 'fought for' as part of the Student Council was the postponing of one of the lectures by half an hour, so that the students who voted for me could get to class on time. My tenure as a student representative only lasted for one term. Between my day job as a full-time journalist and the reading and preparation required by my Master's programme, I was really suffering from a lack of time and inability to take on any additional responsibilities.

This does not mean that working at Student Councils and Unions in Britain is not effective or does not have its benefits. Compared with many Arab student bodies (where they existed), the British were very well advanced. For example, the National Union of Students (NUS), which is a union that brings together 400 students' unions in the UK representing the voices of over seven million students, has been able to achieve a lot of things since its establishment in 1922. Although the Union failed to make Tony Blair's Labour government reverse its decision that put an end to free education and also failed to make David Cameron's Conservative government reverse its decision to raise those fees in 2011,[7] it still is a force to be reckoned with.

In 1992, the Union was also able to exempt all full-time students

---

7 There is more on this in the chapter titled *Great Expectations* in this book.

from paying their Council Tax[8] and provide all students with public transportation cards (including trains and buses) at discounted prices. In 2016, the Union was also able to prove, through the judiciary, that the British Ministry of Interior had deported 48,000 international students by accident due to an unfair English language exam.

Furthermore, many British politicians launch their careers in public service while they are still students, by taking up roles in student organisations such as the National Union of Students. Among them are the former home secretaries Charles Clarke and Jack Straw (who served as Foreign Secretary as well) and Trevor Phillips, who was the first black person to head the NUS and later served as the head of the parliamentary Equality and Human Rights Commission.

It was remarkable for me that, through the innovative teaching methods at Westminster, I was able to graduate with valuable information, credible references, new friends and fond memories. I don't even exclude dry subjects such as Market Research, which was given by one of my all-time favourite lecturers and course leaders, Jon Pike. I remember during his first lecture, he spoke to us about his subject, acknowledging that it is considered less exciting compared with other subjects such as advertising management or public relations. He then started giving us advice on the best ways to study for his subject. I took my pen and copybook and immediately began to write down his advice…but I stopped when he said:

"Conducting market research is like making Spaghetti Bolognese!"

I put my pen down and looked at him with amazement. He continued by saying, with all seriousness, that:

"When we make Bolognese sauce, we need to get tomatoes, onions,

---

8 The Council Tax is a tax that the owner or the tenant of a property pays to the municipality of the area where they live. The value of this tax is set in accordance with the area of the property and the region where it is located in line with pre-set zones. This tax, which is on average £1,200 every year, is used to cover the expenses of cleaning the streets, gathering the rubbish, removing the ice in case of snowfall and so on. As a result of the efforts exerted by the National Union of Students, all those who were able to prove they were full-time students were exempt from paying it.

mushrooms, carrots and minced meat. Ultimately, what defines the quality of the sauce is the quality of these ingredients that we are mixing together. The same thing applies to conducting research, it completely relies on the quality of the ingredients, or information, that we gather."

While I was contemplating — as a writer myself — this metaphor, one of my colleagues raised her hand in objection. She was a very funny young English colleague called Natasha. For a moment, I thought she was going to ask a technical question about research methods, but then she just said:

"But Jon, nobody adds carrots to a Bolognese sauce...where on earth did you get this recipe?"

A long discussion ensued between Jon and Natasha about carrots and what goes into the sauce. I kept looking at them, astonished, before joining the rest of my colleagues in bursting into laughter. I guess we walked out of class with two benefits: we all liked and understood market research a lot better and now knew a whole lot more about the different ways of making pasta!

Among the lecturers was another all-time favourite: former advertising executive and Campaign Management Professor, Trevor Wright. I immediately connected with Trevor, not only because he was incredibly witty and knowledgeable, but he had actually been based in Saudi Arabia for some time. In fact, he had lived in my hometown of Jeddah, and was responsible for some of the most memorable FMCG[9] campaigns during the time he worked with the Binzagr company.[10]

Trevor used to bring a Twix chocolate bar to class every day. The Twix bar went each time to the group that prepared the best creative

---

9 Fast Moving Consumer Goods. FMCG products range from food and drink to toilet paper and pharmaceuticals — any product which is bought regularly by consumers over the counter at relatively low costs.

10 Binzagr is one of the largest distributors of food, drink, beauty, homecare and automotive products in Saudi Arabia, with a history of service of over 130 years. Amongst many global brands, they are the representatives of British company Unilever in the Kingdom.

work or came up with the best marketing campaign idea during his weekly lecture. He used to tell us:

"The Twix bar is only symbolic. The prize might be chocolate today, but it could be an actual award tomorrow."

Both Trevor and Jon became close friends of mine over time, along with several of my classmates such as Paras from India and Hazem Taha who was a Palestinian living in Saudi Arabia. I make sure to meet with them every time I go back to visit London. We still meet at either the Sherlock Holmes Hotel or the Metropolitan Bar — a.k.a. The Met — which is located opposite the University building, right above the entrance to Baker Street station. The Met is where I used to get together with my classmates every Tuesday to talk about our studies, politics, economics and sports.

Similarly to the fictional evening school in Mind Your Language, what was remarkable at Westminster was the multi-nationality of the students, British students being the minority among them. The majority of students in my class were Asians (Chinese, Thai and Indians), followed by students from Russia and Eastern Europe, from Europe (French, Italian, Spanish and so on) a few Americans and of course, African and Arab students.[11]

Naturally, some of my fellow international students fitted into their stereotypes. A Russian classmate was so used to speaking over her mobile during class, that she was even photographed on the phone during the end of term group photo. A Nigerian colleague tried to sell me a 'guaranteed, fast-tracked' British citzenship (but said that he wasn't after one for himself!) An American colleague was, of course, athletic and wore basketball shorts in the cold weather (he liked to act tough!) While the only racist, and dare I say white supremacist, encounter was with an Austrian student. Luckily, I only had to deal with her for one term.

---

11 There are almost 30,000 Middle Eastern students in Britain, with almost 9,000 of those being from Saudi Arabia. Source: https://www.al-fanarmedia.org/2022/11/british-universities-want-more-students-from-the-middle-east/

Since the university's teaching methods required the formation of working groups during the first two weeks, a portion of the final grade was dedicated to the student's ability to work within a group of four or five students and complete the assignments. So, I had to move quickly to choose a group I could adapt to. I did not feel like I belonged to the groups that were quickly and automatically formed between students who already knew each other or those of the same nationality (the Chinese together, the Indians together and so on). In the end, I found myself forming the most unlikely group. But at the same time, I was determined to maximise my learning experience and I was not going to learn anything new if I dealt with the same people I dealt with back home.

My team was diverse. There was Manuella from Italy, who was the Head of Marketing in a digital products company – always very elegant, eloquent and was a very capable leader. Emilie was from France and worked at Transport for London (TFL) – she was full of energy, creative and funny...but, as the French people often do, she objected to almost everything in the beginning! The third member of the team was Ksenia from Lithuania, who used to work in HR. She was always very kind, hardworking and incredibly organised.

Although we became, after several projects, an effective team that consistently came in first place, it took us some time to build the chemistry between us. By the time we graduated, we had all become very close friends and still remain in touch whenever possible.

Our success created some rivalries for us, however, particularly aimed at me from some of the British students. One day, at the beginning of term, one of the lecturers asked us to read a certain book in the library to prepare for the next lecture. So I headed to the university's library, where I ran into a British colleague, who asked me about what I was doing there so late.

I answered her: "Oh, I am here to borrow the book that the lecturer asked us to read before they run out of copies."

Her response was shocking, as she looked at me with resentment, rolled her eyes and said:

"Not everything in life is a competition, Faisal!"

Such comments did not bother me. The principle my team and I agreed to follow was this: it was not a shame for us not to always come in first, but it was a shame not to seek to get there and exert every possible effort to do so.

In this context, a *Daily Mail* report once mentioned that a number of Chinese teachers were blown away when they spent a month at a school in Britain's Hampshire county. They found that British students lacked motivation when compared with their peers in China (who are known for their extreme discipline and competitiveness). According to the newspaper, the Chinese teachers blamed the social security system and assistance provided to unemployed people in Britain for what they described as "the lack of ambition, ill-discipline and idleness" found among British students.[12]

Anyway, back to my team. The relationship between Manuella, Ksenia, Emilie and I evolved from colleagues to friends who exchanged visits and went out to restaurants together. They introduced me to their boyfriends and we are mostly still in touch today.

The years of my Master's programme went by quickly. They taught me how to manage my time more efficiently so that I could balance the requirements of my job and those of my university assignments. I also learned how to reduce my expenses and rationalise them so I could pay the tuition fees. (Incidentally, I once tried to join the Saudi government's student scholarship programme after the late King Abdullah bin Abdul Aziz confirmed the enrolment of students in the delegation would receive state subsidy but unfortunately my university and course were not on the accredited list at the time.)

Here, I must point out how very lucky I was to have been encouraged by a person without whose support I probably would not

---

12 Source: *Daily Mail*, August 2nd, 2015 – https://www.dailymail.co.uk/news/article-3183310/Rude-bone-idle-cosseted-welfare-state-Chinese-teachers-damning-verdict-schoolchildren.html

have been able to finish my Masters programme. This is Dr. Azzam Al-Dakhil,[13] who, at the time, was the CEO of the Saudi Research and Media Group (which owns the *Asharq Al-Awsat* newspaper that I worked for at the time, as well as *Arab News*, where I currently work). Although he was based in Riyadh, he used to visit London for a few days every year and made sure to meet with me and other staff members and motivate us. In time, I formed a close relationship with him and his two sons, Mohammed and Abdullah, who later moved themselves to London to study.

Abu Mohammed (as he liked to be called) was not my direct superior and so was not able to offer me any direct support with my work at the newspaper, but he found an additional work formula that would allow me to pay the tuition fees of my Master's programme. It required me to work overtime for another company affiliated with the group during the weekends and on holidays. His rationale for setting this up was practical: firstly, so that my studies and additional work not interfere with my current job and secondly, so that our group and country would benefit from what I had learned after graduating.

Despite the effort and time it required, this measure helped me cover the university fees (some £11,000 at the time). For this reason I made absolutely sure to invite Dr. Azzam to my graduation ceremony, alongside my family members. He accepted the invitation and attended the ceremony to congratulate me.

After the certificate handover ceremony, I met with my colleagues and professors for the last time as a university student. I was keen to give each of my lecturers, Jon Pike and Trevor Wright, a souvenir gift. I gifted Jon Pike, the Market Research professor I mentioned earlier, a wrapped box which contained a jar of pre-prepared Bolognese sauce with a thank you note that read:

---

13 Dr. Azzam Al-Dakhil was appointed as Education Minister in the Kingdom of Saudi Arabia at the beginning of 2015 after King Salman bin Abdul Aziz ascended to the throne. I was among the first people to congratulate him.

"You may want to tell your future students that, thanks to technology and research companies on the internet, doing market research has become completely instantaneous, just like buying a pre-prepared Bolognese sauce."

As for Trevor, the Advertising Campaign Management professor, he was surprised when he opened his gift. It contained a box inside of a box inside of a box, with the last one containing a Twix chocolate bar and a note on which I wrote the famous sentence he used to repeat during his lectures:

"The Twix bar is only symbolic. The prize might be chocolate today, but it could be an actual award tomorrow!"

In the years that followed, I ended up managing many award-winning advertising campaigns for the newspapers I worked for. My experience serving on the student council was helpful in preparing me to serve as the elected Deputy Chairman of the Saudi Journalist Association in 2024. I also ended up using what I learned in the market research class in my job at *Arab News*, where we partnered with YouGov, a renowned British online polling company, and introduced international-standard political polling into the Saudi press. Our polls are regularly quoted on CNN, Reuters and other agencies.

In 2017, a decade after I first enrolled at Westminster, I won the British Council's UK Alumni Award for Social Impact in Saudi Arabia. I dedicated the award to Jon, Trevor and my colleagues at the University who received me with open arms, and gave me a memorable and incredibly useful experience.

Chapter X

THE WOLF OF SHOREDITCH HIGH STREET

As much as one learns from the years at university, there is nothing that matches a real work experience at a British company to help integrate fully, and to understand your new society better.

As you will have gathered by now, I already had a job in London, and that was as a journalist with *Asharq al-Awsat* newspaper. But while the company that publishes it, Saudi Research and Marketing, was a British-registered company, it was still pretty much predominantly Arab, both in terms of culture and practices.

Of course, working with fellow Arabs had many advantages, such as the feeling of relative security and familiarity, which were both quite important to me at first. But one of the disadvantages was that you — as an immigrant — always feel that you are constantly living in a bubble. You also don't know whether or not you can 'swim' on your own. Sometimes, you never know until someone pushes you into the water!

So I would like to share with you my experience at a Shoreditch

Highstreet-based British publishing company called Ink[1] where I worked as an advertising sales representative for in-flight magazines, between August 2009 and February 2011. With Ink, I ventured into a totally different world, a world far removed from the customs and traditions that define — and sometimes restrict — work environments in many Arab countries.

Of course, it is not like working at Ink was without its issues. Like any workplace, there was rivalry, gossip and at times bad practice. However, compared to my previous workplaces, these all seemed much less significant. Most issues were resolved swiftly and people moved on much quicker at Ink than I had witnessed elsewhere. I am not sure whether it was a matter of Arab vs British culture, Sales vs Editorial or a combination of both.

In comparison, a personal issue would take a very long time to resolve at many Arab companies. If a person brought drama to the office, then most team members would leave what they are doing and focus on patting that person on the shoulder, for hours. If two Arab colleagues got into a heated argument, things would escalate and voices might rise and other people would interfere, whether they were related to the incident or not. What is ironic is, eventually, the fighting parties would probably kiss and make up and return to joking together as if nothing happened except that a day would be needlessly wasted!

In contrast British culture centres on an eagerness to manage time effectively,[2] and people carefully calculate the time they allocate to on

---

1 Established in 1994, its full name until recently was Ink Publishing, but its owners renamed it Ink only because its activities were no longer limited to the mere publication of aviation companies' magazines. The company evolved at one point to deal with everything related to communication with passengers through the medium of advertising. It has moved since its headquarters from Shoreditch High Street to Blackburn Road in North West London.

2 Certainly the matter is relative. The English for example are perceived to be keen on not wasting time compared to Arabs and Latinos, whereas the Germans find the English (and possibly all other human races) disorganised and inefficient in terms of time management, or management as a whole.

any particular task. This is not necessarily a genetic predisposition, or because the care deeply about it, but generally simply because their lifestyle dictates it. If you live far away, for example, you cannot afford to waste time because you wouldn't want to miss your train home. Plus, "there is nothing like a well-earned pint of beer at the pub, after a productive day at the office," as an English friend of mine once told me.

If you look carefully, you will notice that even when your British colleagues moan about topics such as the weather, public transport and the cost of living, they do so without allowing that to impact their productivity. Gossip often happens during a 'water-cooler moment' in which the 'acceptable' time for gossip is limited to the few minutes that employees use to drink water, prepare coffee and tea or smoke in the allocated smoking zones.

This was particularly the case at the very commercially-driven Ink Publishing. This is not a surprise, given that many of the sales managers who worked there used to say:

"You are mistaken if you think that this is a publishing house that does sales; actually, this is a sales house that does publishing."

Now, numbers, targets and key performance indicators (KPIs) may bother some but they are also — if implemented reasonably — incredibly liberating and fair. Such a culture means, by default, that no one cares about the employee's background, religion or their political views as long as he or she achieves the required goals.

To establish this spirit, everyone's goals (both at a team and individual level) were placed on a 'whiteboard' in the middle of the sales floor, and were updated daily according to the progress achieved. There also was a bell ringing every time a team or an individual achieved its goal; all the staff on the floor would respond by clapping, cheering and whistling.

There was a meeting of the sales department twice a week, one at 7.30am on Mondays to set the goals and plans that the various teams would follow, and another at the end of work on Fridays to review what had been achieved. Where did shortcomings occur and how could performance be improved the following week?[3]

In such environments, the role of managers — naturally — is support, enablement and empowerment of their team members. There was little room for egos, because all it took for a manager to fall from hero to zero was missing their target on any particular month.

You might be wondering why this is noteworthy. Well, allow me to say that it was not necessarily the norm in some Arab work cultures at the time. Imagine having to sit through a mind numbing two-hour meeting on a daily basis, and endure the constant praise for the principal from some of your incompetent colleagues who seemed to climb up the professional ladder the more their noses turned brown.

However, it was profit not praise that got you noticed at Ink. Some of the best managers I worked with there were Tony Azouri, Stephan Bartsch and the co-founder of the company, Simon Leslie. Despite Simon's popularity among employees, there were some who accused him of being ruthless, greedy and that all he cared about was money (and he responded to those accusations by saying: "Of course I care about money. If I didn't, we would lose our jobs!")

But whether you liked him or hated him, what you cannot disagree on is that Simon has been able, for nearly three decades, to build and run a successful global company — starting from scratch. Ink is an inspiring story in the publishing world. At one point, it became the largest publisher of inflight magazines in the world. At its peak, it employed 400 people and served 677 million travellers who engaged with its various products.

This global company — which now has offices in Britain, the United States, Asia and Africa — began in 1994 with a modest partnership between two people: Simon Leslie, who ran the sales department and Michael Keating, who took over editorial supervision. Simon

---

3 It should be noted that all the meetings, conducted while standing, took only a few minutes. In the worst cases, it would go up to 15 minutes. No Arab company I had ever worked with by then had meetings which were less than 45 minutes.

often told us how he always had to sell something to survive. In his early days, he worked as a salesman for insurance policies, and then double-glazing for windows, and had to learn how to never accept "no" for an answer.

"I had come back with a deal — at all costs — because if I didn't, my kids would sleep hungry," he used to tell us.

Simon has his own philosophy in life, in which he motivates himself and those working with him and this is how he runs his company. When you go into Ink — specifically on the sales floor — you will find a slogan everywhere that says: "Success is driven by belief." Simon felt that no person could succeed in anything, if he did not want it strongly from the inside and did not believe that he was capable of overcoming obstacles. For this reason he strongly dislikes negative people and defeatist personalities.

Simon was also incredibly likeable; his chubby build and sense of humour may have played a role in making him so endearing to many. I learned from him the importance of 'leadership by example'. This man, despite the wealth he accumulated through his company, which would allow him not to have to work himself, was the first to arrive at work in the morning, often the last to leave in the evening. You would only have to compare that to some of my previous managers who preferred to socialise in hotel lobbies or at events, and then complain that the team was so 'useless' that they had to actually come into the office.

Simon used to sit beside us on the sales floor, not in his own office, which he rarely used. Every Tuesday, he brought us fruit and nuts to motivate us to eat healthy snacks. He personally honoured distinguished members of the team. He enjoyed creating incentive programmes for us and because we worked in the publishing business, he could get very valuable gifts from advertisers free in exchange for discounts or bartered advertising space. Performance incentives ranged from high-end Swiss watches to expensive champagne bottles and fully-paid holidays. Once, one of the top sales teams got a fully paid four-day holiday in Las Vegas, including the cost of the trip and a stay in a five-star hotel.

But what really distinguished Simon was his unique ability to 'rally the troops'. He would enter the Monday morning meeting with people half asleep and leave it with all of us fired up and eager to achieve our goals. His motivational speeches can only be compared to the performance of famous actor Leonardo DiCaprio in the role of American businessman Jordan Belfort in The Wolf of Wall Street.[4] It really seemed like the whole sales floor performance would improve every time Simon gave a speech.

"We don't place caps on the commission you earn here. I want us to write you bigger cheques! Sell more, so that you can achieve your own dreams," he used to tell us.

It was unacceptable for him to delay — for any the reason — commissions owed to sales staff. When this happened once, he cashed the commissions out of his own pocket and then recovered the money from the accounting department after forcing the manager to send an apology to the staff confirming that it would not happen again.

However, as I mentioned earlier, Ink was very strict with those who did not do their job properly. Many of those who did not achieve the required results left the company during the period in which I worked there.[5] In return, he was keen to help those who needed advice, as long as they were willing to work hard.

Once, I remember having a bad month, and I got worried I might be fired. So, I sought Simon's help and I reached out for advice. He agreed to meet me for tea across the street from the company. He asked me what was going on with me and I told him I did not know,

---

4 The Wolf of Wall Street is a 2013 American film directed by Martin Scorsese, starring Leonardo Di Caprio in the role of the famous stockbroker and American businessman Jordan Belfort, who was later jailed on fraud charges. Since his release from prison, Belfort lectures around the world on the selling style he created known as straight line persuasion.

5 Some employees had been criticising the company for some time, saying that it had a quick 'hire and fire' culture, but the contracts were clear and the management's point of view was: a salesperson who doesn't sell is not doing their job.

but I was trying to apply what I learned at university from the basics of marketing, such as choosing the target segment and understanding demography, and then I added:

"I know I am supposed to sell, but clients do not want to listen. Would you believe that a marketing manager at one of the Egyptian resorts I contacted today was more interested in flirting with me on the phone than listening to the pitch?"

Simon burst out laughing and interrupted me saying:

"So flirt with her, man! Faisal, you have to realize that we have hired you because when you talk, you don't sound like a salesman!" He added: "Did you know that we have salespeople who dream of having the necessary confidence to talk to customers comfortably? Why do you want to waste that in giving her boring specs she can read in an email?"

After those tips, Simon reminded me of what I had achieved since I joined the company and said:

"Listen, I never doubted your abilities, but you have to trust yourself. Believe me, you will not get anything in life if you seem weak or hesitant, whether it is closing a client or a dating a girl!"

I left that meeting motivated and in high spirits, and by the end of the day I had closed four deals with different clients. One of those deals was with the marketing manager of the Egyptian Resort, who I contacted again and joked with and complimented for half an hour. Not only did I get a deal from her, but she even offered me a free stay at the resort she ran for three nights any time I visit Egypt. (I take this opportunity to apologise to her for not having been able to take up her generous invitation to this day!)

I dealt with eccentric clients as well, including a customer who owned a real estate company in Lebanon. He objected to something that I would never have imagined could be a problem: in Ink, the initial agreement was made over the phone, then the booking form was sent to the customer to sign and return by fax or e-mail. However, my client said I had to settle for a text message that he would send me by SMS on my mobile phone. He told me that he did not have time for such bureaucratic procedures.

"Do you not know who I am?" he asked, as he threatened to cancel the deal.

I quickly realized he was on an ego trip and that I had to calm him down. So, I told him that — as an Arab — I trusted that the word of such a reputable and accomplished businessman was as good as gold. I then went on a tantrum complaining of all the bureaucracy I had suffered from the day I arrived in the UK, from opening a bank account to being forced to take English language tests for my Master's, when I was perfectly fluent in English. I kept complaining and telling stories until the client burst out laughing when I told him that one day, British couples — out of this country's love for bureaucracy — would have to fill a form, sign it and send it by post to each other before being able to have sex!

The client eventually agreed to sign and send back the form, but closing that deal certainly did feel like pulling teeth!

Of course, this diversity of characters and personalities was not limited only to clients...it extended to the colleagues I worked with. It was certainly funny to compare the actions of my co-workers, from different countries with the stereotypes that were stuck in my mind about those countries.

Claudio was a handsome Italian colleague with soft, long hair. He was a charmer and a 'sweet-talker' by nature. He used to flirt with different girls and make all sorts of romantic promises to them... while he was in the restroom! (Little did they know he was doing so while on a toilet seat, and little did he know, I was in the cabin next door.)

There was Constantin from Romania, who was quite the opposite of Claudio. He was very formal, with short hair, wide shoulders and a deep gaze. His way of selling was very practical and concise, but it was effective because all his clients trusted him blindly.

Mark, a British sales manager, was tall and muscular, resembling

English football star David Beckham in form and modesty. Not only was he a top performer on the sales floor, but he was also very attentive to his looks and style. He used to spend most of his free time in the gym next to the office. He was always dressed up with his tie, his shirt bearing his initials on the sleeve and his golden cufflinks. You weren't surprised if you saw him using deodorant or applying perfume inside the office every few hours.

Naturally, Mark's impeccable looks and confidence impressed most of the ladies at work, while many of the men wanted to be like him. But that didn't go down well with Kevin, his direct line manager and the floor's sales director. Although Kevin used to make funny comments about Mark being a softy, many of us felt he was super-jealous of him. Kevin was a chubby, bald-headed and much older Scot. Many saw him as very tight, not only in terms of money but also with his time and emotion. I don't recall ever seeing him have lunch with anyone, or even eat or have a coffee outside the office. Although he was Simon's deputy, Kevin was quite the opposite in my opinion – his speeches were boring and totally un-inspiring! He was also a penny-counter, he questioned even the smallest of costs, such as mailing our magazines to clients. He asked us to charge them the price of the magazine, even though they had paid thousands of pounds for advertising. Of course, others saw him as wise and efficient — and that the company needed someone who was this careful with spending.

There were many more, like Raphael, the incredibly tall, funny and sweet Frenchman who was also a Judo champion. Then there was Edith, the Eva Longoria lookalike, top-selling Colombian, and Sital who was of Indian origin and constantly exceeded his targets.

Some of my longer serving colleagues at Ink, such as Phil and Tara, have achieved great success and wealth as a result of their working years and the huge commissions they earned selling advertising. As for me, I consider my two-year sales career to be a success in itself. What was remarkable is that this challenge turned out to be mental.

I did not think I could succeed in this profession for two reasons: the first was a complete lack of previous experience, the second and most important reason was my conviction that I would fail because of deeply held beliefs, most of which later proved to be wrong.

First of all, as a career journalist, I had a false feeling that I was 'above' working in sales. Then, there was the preconceived idea we had in the Arab world that some nationalities, such as the Lebanese and the Egyptians, were gifted and better salespeople. Then, there was also the belief in our culture that livelihood is predestined or 'written'. In other words, I was afraid to work hard without achieving the desired result, if that result was not predestined.

But the surprise for me was when, thanks to Ink's management, I went from someone with little confidence in his ability to succeed, to someone thinking about how to develop the company as a whole and add more success to it. Of course, this also has to do with the power of working in sales. Suddenly, I was no longer working at a Cost Centre, but at a Profit Centre, and this came with many advantages and much influence.

One of the development ideas I endorsed was for Voyager magazine, which was distributed on board British Midland International (BMI)[6] aircraft in the Arab world. The magazine considered itself a classy lifestyle publication, with celebrities such as George Clooney and Beyoncé always the cover story. But the magazine's coverage of Arab destinations was boring and weak.

For me, this was a challenge and an exciting opportunity. I wanted the content of a magazine like this, read by tens of thousands of international travellers every month, to keep abreast of the story of the development of our region. The only obstacle was that the magazine had a one-dimensional, and incredibly boring British editor-in-chief at the time.

---

6 British Midland International (BMI) was a United Kingdom airline company flying from the United Kingdom to Europe, the Middle East, North America and Central Asia. It was part of the Sky Alliance from 2000 until British Airways bought it in April 2012.

Because she had previously worked for a fashion magazine, she was fixated with luxury brands and meeting international fashion designers. She paid no attention to the Arab world, of which her knowledge was probably limited to the One Thousand and One Nights stories.[7]

Of course, this was affecting me directly: with such an editorial line, I was struggling to win over Arab advertisers. I explained to the management the importance and reasons for the presence of figures such as Queen Rania of Jordan and Sheikha Moza from Qatar (this was before Sheikh Hamad bin Khalifa II stepped down in 2013 in favour of his son Sheikh Tamim) on the covers of these magazines and the positive impact on perception, reputation and the volume of advertisements. What also helped was that BMI was originally planning at that time (2009-2010) to stop travel to Tel Aviv, increase flights to Syria and Egypt, as well as open a new line to Libya and also travel to Jordan, Egypt, Lebanon and Saudi Arabia.

Ink also had a first-rate professional editorial director, and because the company was commercially driven, the attitude was that the proof has to be in the pudding.

Luckily, the success of this new strategy was immediate. When Queen Rania was on the cover of BMI Voyager magazine in July 2010, Jordanian newspapers wrote about the interview and representatives of some embassies and cultural destinations contacted us asking for a number of copies. This was certainly due to the fact that Queen Rania — with her diverse achievements — was a unique model and the story broke the stereotype of Arab women. It was indisputable that major companies in Jordan such as local telecommunications companies, banks and prominent tourism facilities called us to

---

7 *One Thousand and One Nights*, also known in the West as *The Arabian Nights*, is a collection of stories from the Middle East going back probably to the eighth century, with the first stories originating in India and Persia. The first English translation appeared in the early eighteenth century. In the collection, the ruler Shahryar is told the stories by his wife Scheherazade.

advertise with us. Even British fashion designer Bruce Oldfield (who designed Queen Rania's wedding dress in 1993), advertised with us and his marketing team asked for the page next to her interview.[8]

During the Christmas holidays in December 2010, I travelled to spend the holidays with my family carrying all sorts of gifts and happy with the success — and income — I had achieved thanks to my new job with Ink. I also remember being excited about the New Year, telling myself that it would be a busy and successful year.

Of course, 2011 did end up being a busy year...but in a way that no-one had expected.

One night during the holiday season, I saw what I thought would be a fleeting news item about a young Tunisian man (later identified as Mohamed Bouazizi) who set himself on fire in the town of Sidi Bouzid. I did not imagine that this spark would, in just weeks, trigger what was later known as the 'Arab Spring'. And little did I know that I was going to be among its first victims...

---

8 Some advertisers can demand a certain place to advertise in the magazine, with the right-hand side (in English magazines written from left to right) usually being more expensive; pages facing exclusive interviews of this kind are usually more expensive. Among the costliest pages are the back cover, the inside back cover and the inside front cover.

CHAPTER XI

ABSENT IN THE SPRING

Undoubtedly, the year 2011 was a turning point in modern Arab history. It is a year which saw unexpected change that still impacts the Middle East and North Africa to this day. These winds of change eventually became known as the Arab Spring.[1]

As determined protesters took to the streets, and anger swept the region, it was not long before the first casualties took place: Tunisian President Zine El-Abidine Ben Ali,[2] his Egyptian counterpart

---

1 The Arab Spring marked a transformative period characterized by a wave of anti-government protests, uprisings, and armed rebellions that swept through much of the Arab world in the early 2010s. Originating in Tunisia as a response to widespread corruption and economic stagnation, the movement swiftly to spread and met with success in five other nations: Libya, Egypt, Yemen, Syria, and Bahrain. There were failed attempts in several Arab countries.

2 Zine El-Abidine Ben Ali (1936-2019) held the position of second president of Tunisia from 1987 until 2011. His tenure abruptly ended amidst the Tunisian revolution of that year, leading to his ousting and subsequent exile in Saudi Arabia. Ben Ali's ascent to power had begun with his earlier appointment to Prime Minister in October 1987. He then seized the presidency on November 7, 1987, following a bloodless coup d'état that deposed President Habib Bourguiba on grounds of incompetence.

Muhammad Hosni Mubarak[3]...and yours truly!

By February, it was clear that my short-lived career in advertising sales was over. Essentially, my clients — who were all based in affected countries — were dropping out and cancelling their ad bookings, one major spender after the other. Industries such as travel, tourism and real estate were among the first to feel the pinch. Not only that, but the airlines which carried the in-flight magazines that I worked with had decided to completely cancel routes to impacted cities, or to reduce them significantly.

But rather than being like an Arab dictator who lived in denial and defied the will of the people, I opted to bow out when senior management told me my job was no longer sustainable. I left on great terms and, within a week, started another job as a Senior Middle East Correspondent for a (now defunct) monthly called the *International Resource Journal* (IRJ). My transition was a lot easier given that I now had spent enough years and paid enough taxes to obtain Indefinite Leave to Remain, which gave me the freedom to change jobs as I wished.[4]

However, as happy as I was to have joined a new London-based magazine, and as important as the energy story was (and still is), I was suffering a severe case of FOMO.[5] As I watched dramatic events

---

3 Muhammad Hosni El Sayed Mubarak (1928-2020) held the position of the fourth president of Egypt from 1981 to 2011. Before politics, Mubarak had built a career as an officer in the Egyptian Air Force, ultimately serving as its commander from 1972 to 1975 and attaining the rank of Air Chief Marshal in 1973. In 1975 he was appointed Vice President by President Anwar Sadat. Following Sadat's assassination in 1981, Mubarak assumed the presidency. Mubarak's presidency endured for nearly three decades, marking one of the lengthiest tenures in Egypt's modern history.

4 Indefinite Leave to Remain (ILR) is a visa stamped on the passport of immigrants to Britain who meet the requirements of the Immigration Department after a certain number of years. In my case, I got it because I had been residing, working and paying taxes regularly for five years. 'Permanent Residency' gives expatriates all the rights that citizens enjoy, except voting and the right to obtain a passport. This means that they can live in Britain permanently, they can enter and leave the country whenever they please, and it also removes any restrictions when it comes to getting a job or studying in universities.

5 FOMO: popular expression, being an abbreviation of Fear Of Missing Out.

unfold in Tunis, Cairo, Manama, Damascus and other Arab cities, I felt I was… Absent in the Spring! Just as Agatha Christie's character Joan Scudamore[6] found herself unexpectedly alone, stranded between trains and compelled to self-reflect, I, too, had to re-examine my priorities, passions and personality.

I now lived a comfortable life in the UK, I had a few close friends, many social circles and I finally felt settled in. But something was missing, and that something was: Purpose!

What further ignited this feeling was that the year 2011 refused to slow down. In May, the world — which was already struggling to keep up with the change happening in the Middle East — woke up to another major headline which would change modern history: the US killing of Al-Qaeda's leader, Osama bin Laden.[7]

Deep inside, I knew I needed to go back to the Middle East and I knew I needed to go back into covering politics. Alas, there was no immediate opportunity, so I decided to double down on my writing on regional developments. I had my job with the the IRJ as one outlet. But I was lucky enough to have another which gave me a lot more freedom of choice when it came to topics, and unmatched

---

6 *Absent in the Spring* is a novel written by Agatha Christie in 1944, writing for a while under the pseudonym Mary Westmacott. Christie is one of the most famous crime novelists in the world and her work has been translated into hundreds of languages and has sold millions of copies. The novel is about a fictional character, Joan Scudamore, who, upon her return from visiting her daughter in Iraq, encounters an unforeseen predicament: she becomes marooned and isolated in a remote rest house due to flooding of the railway tracks. This abrupt solitude serves as a catalyst for Joan to embark on a profound introspection, prompting her to confront the realities of her life with newfound clarity.

7 Osama bin Laden, who was a Saudi before he was stripped of his citizenship, was the main suspect in the attacks of September 11th, 2001 and was the number one wanted man in the world for 10 years before being executed on May 2nd, 2011 in his secret residential complex in Abbottabad, Pakistan by a US Special Forces unit. In 2023, *The Guardian* published a story about bin Laden's 'Letter to America' which was removed from social media by the TikTok organisation: https://www.theguardian.com/technology/2023/nov/16/tiktok-bin-laden-letter-to-america-videos-removal

exposure when it came to reach: *The Huffington Post.*[8]

My story with the *HuffPo* (as its fans like to call it) started back in 2008. I was still working with *Asharq al-Awsat* at the time, but I had a growing fascination with the English language and was keen to explore opportunities to write in English. I decided to set up my own WordPress blog, called *Media: an International Arab Perspective,* where I would both translate my Arabic stories from *Asharq al-Awsat* and also write original content in English — including commentary — as an experiment and a way to practice.

Months later, I got an email from Hannah, the newly appointed international editor at *HuffPo*. She was adamant about recruiting me to write for them. When I asked asked her for the terms and conditions, her answer was a journalist's fantasy: there were no deadlines, no word counts and nothing I couldn't write about. The catch, though, was the fourth item which was: there was no payment — something I didn't appreciate, but decided to accept nevertheless given the massive reach I would be getting. Little did I know, that was going to be one of the best investments in my life.

Shortly after I started writing for *HuffPo*, I won a Cutting Edge Award from the London-based Next Century Foundation. This award was given to me in recognition of my work's contribution

---

8 *The Huffington Post* is a prominent American progressive news website boasting both localised and international editions. Its diverse content offerings include news, satire, blogs, and original pieces covering a wide array of topics such as politics, business, entertainment, environment, technology, and much more. In 2012, the website achieved a significant milestone by becoming the first commercially run digital media enterprise in the United States to receive a Pulitzer Prize. There always was, however, some controversy about the fact that the company didn't pay writers; see this from Forbes magazine in 2011: https://www.forbes.com/sites/tjwalker/2011/02/12/how-much-did-arianna-huffington-make-and-is-it-fair-her-writers-made-nothing/?sh=48cd5ca54270

bridging the communication gap between the East and the West.[9]

Of course, this was not an Oscar or a BAFTA, but still, to be recognised with an award, and then congratulated and commended publicly by the likes of Lord Stone of Blackheath, Professor Adrian Monck of London's City University's journalism school, *Huffington Post* founder Arianna Huffington and veteran *Washington Post* columnist Jim Hoagland was a badge of honour which I still am proud of today.

And so, to compensate for my absence during this historic period in the Middle East, I decided to double down on my writing for *HuffPo*. I also decided to double down on my participation in entities such The Frontline Club[10] in Paddington and the Foreign Press Association (FPA),[11] which was headed at the time by the late (and great) Egyptian journalist Hosni Imam. My activities with the FPA included being selected as a member of the jury that judged the

---

9 The Foundation is non-profit organisation established in London in 1990 that works to organise dialogues and find solutions to some regional conflicts, especially the Israeli-Palestinian conflict. The list of conflicts that the organisation seeks to contribute to resolving includes Iraq, Syria, Kashmir, Kosovo, Libya, Egypt and Yemen. Through its Press and Broadcasting Council, which seeks to spread and encourage best and ethical media practices, NCF organises an annual competition called the International Press Awards. Among the most notable winners of this competition over the years are Mr. Abdul Rahman Al-Rashed (a lifetime achievement award); Roula Khalaf, Middle East editor of the British *Financial Times*; Ian Black, Middle East editor of *The Guardian* (received the 'Peace through the Media' award); and my colleague Ayman Mohyeldin, an ex-correspondent of the British *Al-Jazeera* channel and now with MSNBC, who received the 'Cutting Edge' award in 2011.

10 Established by Vaughan and Pranvera Smith, the Frontline Club is a distinguished media club and registered charity close to Paddington Station in London. Renowned for its unwavering commitment to conflict reporting, the club serves as a bastion of independent journalism, advocating for diversity and professionalism within the media landscape. The Frontline Club endeavours to foster a safe and conducive environment for journalists, promoting ethical practices while championing the principles of press freedom and freedom of expression on a global scale. Through its initiatives and activities, the club seeks to elevate the discourse surrounding media integrity and accountability, serving as a vital hub for journalists and media professionals alike.

11 The Foreign Press Association, located in St James's Square in London, is the first and oldest association of foreign journalists in the world, founded in 1888. It provides official journalistic accreditation to more than 2,500 international correspondents every year.

2008 annual awards, which took place that year under the patronage of the then Prince of Wales (now King Charles), on the occasion of the 120th anniversary of the association's founding at the Sheraton Park Lane Hotel.

As a member of the jury, I had the honour of receiving an audience with the Prince of Wales during a cocktail reception ahead of the event. It was the first time I had met His Royal Highness; I still remember going to hire a black-tie suit and practicing how to address him days before the encounter. However, my anxiety about committing a faux pas quickly vanished, as Prince Charles had such a comforting humility to him. I warmly remember exchanging small talk and he made us all laugh with his sharp wit and sense of humour.

As the only Arab on the judging committee, I once again felt like a basket of exotic fruit, but this time it was due to interest in my background. His Royal Highness was fascinated to learn that I was from Saudi Arabia, where I knew for a fact he had longstanding and deep friendships with many of our own royals.[12] He asked me about the judging process. I quickly responded with the seriousness that I would have employed when responding to a senior Arab official: "I am sure you will find our selection of winning journalists satisfactory, your Royal Highness."

Prince Charles smiled and said, with some sarcasm, "Oh, I wouldn't have the slightest idea."

He then went on to deliver a fascinating speech on the importance of preserving nature. I still remember his opening lines, where he raised a laugh by saying:

"The FPA is twice as old as I am and doubtless in better shape after celebrating its 120th anniversary than I am after my 60th."

I leaned in heavily on my FPA colleagues in 2011, along with the other contacts and sources I had got to know during my time

---

12 Not many people know that the then Prince Charles held a joint painting exhibition called 'Painting and Care' in Riyadh in 2001 in association with Prince Khalid Al Faisal, son of the late King Faisal of Saudi Arabia: https://www.arabnews.com/node/213132

in London covering the Arab Spring remotely. I managed to score a number of exclusives, including a sit-down interview in London with Wael Ghonim, who was the face of the Egyptian revolution.[13] In London, I also interviewed Abdel Latif Al Menawy, who was Head of News at Egypt's state television and documented the last days of the Mubarak regime. And I achieved another exclusive with a commander at the Syrian Electronic Army who had shot to fame when his group hacked the emails and social media accounts of the Dubai-based pan-*Arab news*caster, Al Arabiya News Channel.

I doubled down on giving commentary to CNN, BBC and Sky News and I spoke to a number of British newspapers. Many of the conversations were super-interesting; on rare occasions, I had disputes about either misinformed or inaccurate reporting. I once got the *Financial Times* to publish a correction after it misquoted me, but that took nearly four months of back and forth with them. However, my favourite story was back in 2008, when the famous shoe throwing incident happened to former US President George W Bush when he visited Iraq.[14]

I remember a BBC journalist ringing me for some background:

"Faisal, what does throwing a shoe at someone mean in Arab culture?"

You can only imagine my surprise. I recall answering along the lines of:

---

13 Wael Ghonim is a computer engineer who, in 2011, rose to international prominence by playing a pivotal role in igniting pro-democracy protests in Egypt. His impassioned interview following 11 days of clandestine detention by Egyptian authorities served as a catalyst for widespread demonstrations. During his time in detention, Ghonim faced intense interrogation regarding his involvement as one of the administrators of the Facebook page 'We are all Khaled Said,' a platform instrumental in catalysing the Egyptian Revolution of 2011. Ghonim's influential role during the uprising made him famous all over the world, and *Time* magazine honoured him by including him in its prestigious 'Time 100' list of the most influential people in 2011.

14 Iraqi journalist Muntazer al-Saidi gained fame for hurling his shoes at the President in a news conference to show his fury at the chaos following the US invasion. Source: Reuters, 2023:   https://www.reuters.com/world/middle-east/no-regrets-iraqi-who-threw-his-shoes-bush-2023-03-14/

"Well, unless there is a shoe fetish thing going on, throwing a shoe at someone is pretty much a universal insult, and a serious security violation given that it was the US President on the receiving end."

There were also some disputes I had with the British media in August of 2011. When protesters took to the streets in London and other UK cities as a rejection of police brutality towards black people, they were mostly peaceful, calling for accountability and equality. They enjoyed a lot of solidarity and support at the beginning. Some even began to call it the UK's Arab Spring moment. But then when protests turned violent and involved damaging public property and looting trainers and electronic gadgets from shops, one began to wonder: what does that have to do with police brutality? (In a way, it was very similar to a question Piers Morgan asked a vegan activist nearly twenty years later: what did disfiguring a national monument like Big Ben have to do with convincing meat-eaters to stop eating meat?

However, what made me happy is that many of the commentators who appeared on British channels were quick to refute the idea that this unrest in Britain could be compared to what was happening in the 'Arab Spring.' *The Guardian* featured a comment that said:

"I think it's insulting to compare the Egyptian uprising, which was entirely political with clear goals, to a bunch of poor angry youths in London stealing trainers."[15]

After all, for all its faults, the British system still provided free education, healthcare and housing to all, as well as stipends to those in need. These rights might not be enough or might be taken for granted by the angry British teenagers who stole Nike shoes and Apple products, but to millions around the world, these rights were ALL they aspired to.

As events continued to unfold, I received invitations to speak from prominent universities such as the School of Oriental and African

---

15 Source: The *Guardian* Newspaper, 9th August 2011: https://www.theguardian.com/uk/2011/aug/09/uk-riots-egyptians-swap-views

Studies at the University of London (SOAS), the London School of Economics (LSE) and the highly prestigious Cambridge Union Society (CUS).

At CUS, I was invited to a debate which was held in February 2012 on the occasion of the first anniversary of the 'Arab Spring.' The debate was titled: "This house believes that the Arab Spring is a threat to global stability."

As I looked over the list of eminent British and international speakers who had been invited to present their views at CUS over a period of more than two centuries,[16] I couldn't but laugh as I recalled how my biggest achievement to date was a heated debate with a McDonald's branch manager over ketchup, when I first arrived in London eight years before.

At 30 (my age at the time), I believed I had come a long way, and for good reason too. Here I was debating at the same venue which had hosted former British Prime Ministers such as Winston Churchill, Margaret Thatcher and John Major. This was in addition to US Presidents Theodore Roosevelt and Ronald Reagan, the former Iraqi President Jalal Talabani and former German Chancellor Helmut Kohl. Among other speakers at CUS were great thinkers such as the Dalai Lama, British scientist Stephen Hawking, founder of 'WikiLeaks' Julian Assange, in addition to actors Clint Eastwood, Roger Moore, Judi Dench, Pamela Anderson as well as prominent journalists, academics, ambassadors and public figures.

For those who are not aware of the rules of engagement at both the Cambridge and Oxford Unions, they resemble what occurs in British Parliament sessions held in the Palace of Westminster in London. The speakers are divided into two opposing groups — opposition and proposition — and a vote is taken among the attending audience at the end of the debate.

---

16 The Cambridge Union Society was founded in 1815. Although this association bears the name 'Union,' it is not a student union as is the case with the National Union of Students (NUS), but rather a 'Union' in the sense of being integrated in Student Debating Societies.

I decided to be in favour of the side that that argued that the 'Arab Spring' harmed global stability. What made me take that stance was that this debate took place a year after the beginning of the revolutions and the intervening period had given me time to reflect. While I, like many others, was taken at first by the events and saw hope in them, it became clear that the international community was mishandling the situation; the Syrian people, for example, were not going to be protected and the region would become a fertile ground for extremism (which it eventually did a few years later with the creation of Daesh.)[17]

I adopted the view that the generation that was seeing its families and relatives getting killed while the world was watching, would not forgive our silence.

Despite strong counter-arguments from the opposition side, I clung to my position and actually did not change it until a member of my own team spoke with an utterly unacceptable logic. He was member of a British think tank called the Henry Jackson Society, which is described as a neo-conservative organisation.[18]

At first, I agreed with my honourable colleague that liberalism must be a basis for democracy, so that elections will not be misused in order to bring to power undemocratic groups (such as Hamas, Hezbollah and the Muslim Brotherhood) which hijack revolutions in order to impose their ideological agendas. I totally disagreed with

---

17 Daesh, also known in the West as ISIS, is a jihadist group which gained global notoriety in 2014 when its militants successfully seized large swathes of territory in northwest Iraq and eastern Syria, exploiting the turmoil of the Syrian civil war. By the end of 2015, it controlled an area inhabited by almost 12 million people, managing an annual budget of over US$12bn and commanding a force of over 30,000 fighters. After protracted fighting with American, Iraqi and Kurdish forces, Daesh lost control of all its Middle Eastern territories by 2019.

18 The Henry Jackson Society is a trans-Atlantic think tank dedicated to foreign policy and national security, headquartered in the United Kingdom, and named in honour of the US Senator and leading Democrat, Henry M. Jackson. While positioning itself as non-partisan, its ideological stance has been characterised as right-wing, neoliberal, and neoconservative. It was founded in 2005 by academics and students at Cambridge University.

him on his depiction of Arabs and Muslims, and his views that we cannot be trusted. He went on to argue that the only way to spread democracy is by military might, such as what occurred in Iraq.

As soon as he finished his intervention, I got up from my chair, requested permission to speak and told the CUS President (who acts as the Speaker of the House during these sessions) that I could no longer sustain being in proposition if it was on the grounds that were just mentioned by my colleague from the Henry Jackson Society.

I walked across the hall towards the opposition side, and suddenly a round of applause swept across the hall. Then one of the opposition speakers stood up and shook my hand firmly; it was British MP Jeremy Corbyn (who I did not know at the time, but in 2015 he became the leader of the opposition Labour Party and its candidate to be elected as Prime Minister!)

As expected, the vote fell — especially after my dramatic scene — in favour of the opposition. My new side won by an overwhelming majority of 291 votes to only 36 who voted in favour of the 'Arab Spring' being a threat to global security, while 98 abstained. As we left the hall, CUS's vice-president of the club approached me and said:

"Mr. Abbas, I think you just made history!"

He explained that in the long history of the debating club, nobody had ever switched sides and that this was a first that would be remembered.

Less than two weeks after that session, I received a thank-you note from the club presidency in the mail. They also decided to grant me an honorary life membership (although I am not a student or alumnus of the University of Cambridge) entitling me to enter the building, use all its facilities at any time and attend all future discussions.

So by mid 2012, with all the work and talks I was doing, I finally thought I had found purpose. It was not too long after that before a dramatic opportunity presented itself. This happened during my visit to Dubai, in May of 2012, when I was attending the Arab Media

Forum (AMF). Among the people I met there was Abdulrahman Al Rashed, General Manager of Al Arabiya News Channel.

As mentioned earlier, I had interviewed a member of the Syrian Electronic Army who had hacked Al Arabiya's social media accounts, and published the story on *The Huffington Post*. What I didn't publish — on ethical grounds — was all the extra details, photos and secrets obtained by the hacker, which he shared with me as evidence that he was, indeed, one of the perpetrators. So when I met Al Rashed at the AMF, I explained that I had a file that I would like to hand over to him in person, containing the above-mentioned documents. He invited me over to his office the next day at the Al Arabiya headquarters in Dubai Media City.

I handed over the file, explaining what it contained. He smiled gently, and asked why I had not published what was in it.

"I just thought it was unethical: it didn't add anything to the story nor was it in the public interest to share illegally obtained personal photos of your presenters," I responded.

The meeting was meant to be short, but we ended up talking for over an hour and a half. We spoke about everything from life in the UK — he used to be a Londoner himself and a former editor of *Asharq al-Awsat* — to regional geopolitics and the news industry. I had no idea that by the end of that meeting, I was going to walk out 'knighted': I was offered, and I immediately accepted, a position as the new Editor-in-Chief of Al Arabiya English, the English language service of the newscaster. The bad news was, I had a month to pack up and move from London to Dubai.

As soon as I landed back in the UK, I resigned from my job at *The International Business Journal*, started selling my furniture and prepared for my move to Dubai. As I went through my papers and packed my belongings, I remembered my first days in London, when I used to walk alone along Oxford Street, looking for somebody to talk to and befriend. I stood in front of the Master's degree that decorated my wall, along with the Cutting Edge Award and the

Honorary membership of the Cambridge Union Society. However, the moment of truth was when I started making a list of friends and colleagues I wanted to invite to my farewell party. As the list was long and my apartment was small, I ended up having three different parties, one every weekend, and invited 20 to 25 friends to each.

Among the invitees were Arab, British and European friends. On the list were also my professors and close colleagues from Westminster University, along with lawyers, diplomats, artists and fellow journalists from Arab and British media outlets.

During each of these farewell parties, I gathered my guests and told the same line before we going on to enjoy a final BBQ in the garden of my Fulham flat (the one by Brompton Cemetery, which still scared me):

"Dear friends, when I came to London in 2004, I had no friends and only had a small sum of money. Tonight, as I prepare to leave this beautiful but expensive city, I have even less money but I am proud to say I leave with more friends that I could have ever imagined!"

As my guests ate and drank through the night, I couldn't help but admire how this city had brought us all so closely together, despite our multicultural backgrounds and different ethnicities. They were all successful Londoners, and then it hit me: I too was now something of a successful Londoner. Yes, I didn't become a mayor like Sadiq Khan managed to do a few years after I left, nor did I become as rich as the late Egyptian Londoner, Mr. Al Fayed. But then again, you simply don't measure your success based on a comparison to others, you base it on a comparison of where you were, and where you are now.

I know I said in the opening chapter of this book that I enjoy English humour, religiously read the British press and occasionally indulge in a scone or two with my afternoon tea; but these are not the things that make me an Anglophile. In fact, what makes me admire and respect this country is nothing material. Remember, the dreaded Abu Hamza (a.k.a. 'Captain Hook') is a naturalised citizen with a British passport, yet he loathed Britain and worked against it.

It is also not the university degree that I obtained, as there are about 900,000 graduates who get one every year. I could also go to the pub, drink beer and watch football if I liked, but remember, almost every tourist does that the moment they set foot in the UK.

No, what made me an Anglophile — as you must have guessed by now — is the amazing experiences I lived, valuable lessons I learned, and great people I describe in this book. I respect this country because it taught me the value of time and money. I admire it because most people I met on the way saw where I was headed, and decided to help, rather than get in the way. I am grateful because it moulded me to become punctual, precise and practical. It made me more independent, determined and decisive.

It was also the respect, tolerance and social justice that I experienced here, even as the country was undergoing its worst terrorist attack it has seen in its modern history. All of this made me leave in awe and gratitude.

As I boarded the overnight Emirates Airlines from Heathrow to Dubai on 15th July 2012, I sat back and reflected on all that I had experienced. I closed my eyes and thought: I had arrived here with a dream of being taken seriously as a journalist, and now I am departing to become the Editor-in-Chief of the English service of the most respected pan-Arab news channel there is.

I did start the book off by saying in Chapter One that you should always be careful what you wish for, as wishes may come true…but hard work, discipline and the willingness to take the plunge also helps. Was I nervous walking into the newsroom as Editor-in-Chief the very next day? Of course, but then again, one just has to Keep Calm and Carry On, right?

EPILOGUE

A TALE OF TWO KINGDOMS

Time just flies, doesn't it? 2024 marks twenty years since I first moved to London. How do I look back at it? Well, in the words of Charles Dickens, I would say: "It was the best of times, it was the worst of times...it was the Spring of Hope, it was the Winter of Despair."[1]

I also had both everything and nothing before me, all in a span of eight unforgettable years. In retrospect, I would now say that it was a 'far, far better thing that I did' than I had ever done!

The previous chapters describe in great detail my journey, lessons learnt and transition from an anglophone to anglophile. You will notice I speak candidly of my mishaps, as I do of my successes. After all, one of the most notable definitions of 'experience' is that it is an accumulation of one's mistakes. Together, both my mishaps and successes have shaped my impressions of Great Britain. But one must

---

1 The famous opening lines from *A Tale of Two Cities* by Charles Dickens: "It was the best of times, it was the worst of times, it was the age of wisdom, it was the age of foolishness, it was the epoch of belief, it was the epoch of incredulity, it was the season of Light, it was the season of Darkness, it was the spring of hope, it was the winter of despair."

remember, while facts are stubborn things, impressions can be fluid and are circumstantial.

I say this because much can change over two decades. This is why I am thankful that my original plan of publishing an immediate and straightforward translation of the original 2017 Arabic edition of this book was delayed. It was far more interesting to revisit, rewrite and reflect on each and every chapter. The delay was a blessing in disguise.

How much has changed? A lot! Neither I, nor anyone, could have predicted the magnitude of changes that have occurred in the past twenty years. Some were positive, such as what is currently happening in my home country, the Kingdom of Saudi Arabia. Some changes were unfortunately not terribly good, such as what went on in my adopted home, the United Kingdom, which I left in 2012.

I returned to Saudi Arabia in 2016, after being appointed as the Editor-in-Chief of *Arab News*. It wouldn't be an exaggeration to say the Kingdom has been living through a period of national transformation that has made it unrecognisable compared to what it was less than a decade ago. This is as true for you, a reader who has picked up this book in London or ordered on Amazon, as it is for me: a local and a journalist whose job it is to keep track of these changes.

Since 2016, I have witnessed and reported on the bold reforms that swept through Saudi Arabia as part of Crown Prince Mohammed bin Salman's Vision 2030. The change includes completely stripping away the previously unchecked powers of the notorious religious police; the Kingdom now enjoys social freedoms and more religious tolerance than ever before. As it stands, there is an open invitation to the Archbishop of Canterbury to visit.

Women, who until 2018 were not even allowed to drive, now enjoy equal rights to men after the abolition of the previous draconian and outdated laws that discriminated against them. As a result, female participation in the workforce has risen from 19% in 2016 to more than 36% in 2023. We now have female ambassadors, soldiers, business executives, footballers as well as astronauts. Rayyanah Barnawi, became the first female Arab/Muslim to travel to the International Space Station last year. If all goes well, female participation alone is expected to boost the country's economy by $39 billion, or 3.5%, by 2032 assuming the current rate of growth continues, according to S&P Global Ratings.[2]

This year, we celebrated the 100 million tourist benchmark, originally set as a target for the Saudi Ministry of Tourism for 2030. Our revived national football league is now among the most watched in the world, with international superstars such as Christiano Ronaldo and Neymar Jr. residing in Riyadh and playing for competing clubs there. During the last World Cup in Qatar, the Saudi National football team was the only team to defeat the reigning World Champions, Argentina, in an unforgettable match that left everyone singing "Don't cry for me, Argentina!"[3]

Did these changes please everyone? Of course not. Naturally, painful mistakes also occurred, and a hefty price was paid for them. Mistakes, sometimes terrible, do happen. Could I be a bit biased towards my home country? Perhaps, but that doesn't negate the numbers above, nor the overwhelmingly positive vibe sweeping across Saudi Arabia. Just ask the thousands of new expats who have migrated to our capital city, Riyadh, how safe, better off and welcome they feel. Or better yet, ask Ipsos, who have named us — Saudis — the second happiest people in the world in 2023.[4]

One of the reasons why Vision 2030 has been a success so far in Saudi Arabia is that it was honest that with reform, there will be pain sometimes. One of the examples is raising the VAT from 5% to 15% back in 2020. The other aspect, of course, is that given our political

---

2 Source: *Fast Company*, September 2023: https://fastcompanyme.com/news/more-women-in-saudi-workforce-could-add-39-billion-to-economy-says-sp/

3 The famous song written by Andrew Lloyd Webber and Tim Rice for their 1978 musical *Evita*.

4 Source: *Arab News*, March 2023: https://www.arabnews.com/node/2272011/saudi-arabia

system — which again is not perfect — guarantees continuity given that policy makers are thinking long-term, rather than only as far as the next election.

Perhaps in due course, another book could discuss the Saudi transformation in more detail.

But then again, this is not a book about Saudi Arabia. This is a book about the United Kingdom which in 2024, ranked — in ironic contrast — as "the second most miserable nation in the world."[5]

How did the UK get there? It is undoubtedly a fall from grace for a country which I, like many others of my age back in 2004, regarded as such a wonderful place that I actually equated getting a work permit to come and work here to winning the golden ticket in Charlie and the Chocolate Factory!

Perhaps fellow British journalists, socioeconomic experts and anthropologists can better explain what happened more accurately. Some might disagree with me, and argue that the situation is actually, not that bad. Others will say that UK still enjoys unique cultural, historical and educational aspects.

Like many countries around the world, British politics — in my opinion — has fallen victim to populism. Of course, while both the public and an elected official's constituency must be respected, it is dangerous for politicians to feel their every word is being judged as if they are on an episode of the X Factor. This is unfortunately the case with the widespread, and real time, intrusion of social media. As renowned *New York Times* columnist Thomas Friedman, author of the best-selling book, *That Used To Be US: How America Fell Behind The World It Invented And How We Can Come Back,* described it to me once: "There are three of us in the room now: me, my audience and weaponised social media."

This is especially evident in Western democracies, where politicians

5 The rating came from an American analysis of mental health in countries around the world. Source: *Daily Telegraph*, March 2023: https://www.telegraph.co.uk/travel/destinations/europe/united-kingdom/mental-wellness-index-uk-miserable-nation/

have declined from the class and calibre of the late Senator John McCain who opted to defend his competitor, Barack Obama, back in 2008 when confronted by a racist voter. He told her: "No ma'am, he's a decent family man, citizen, that I just happen to have disagreements with on fundamental issues, and that's what this campaign is all about."[6]

US politics has gone from there to politicians who publicly demean women by saying things like "grab 'em" by a particularly intimate body part. Both political parties are equally guilty in reaching such a polarised situation, and it is one that now divides America, paralyzing decision-making and delaying much-needed reforms.

In the UK, we have noticed this same phenomenon. In the Captain Hook chapter of this book, I recall how reassured and safe I felt as a new immigrant when I heard Sir Ian Blair, who was head of the London Metropolitan Police at the time, refuse to be dragged into calling Muslims terrorists after the 7/7 attacks of 2005. He went so far as to say in a Parliamentary Select Committee: "Our particular object is to do this: to make the Muslim communities [of Britain] feel protected and to assist them."[7]

I was also surprised when I heard a speech by now former Foreign Secretary William Hague delivered during the International Institute for Strategic Studies (IISS) Manama Dialogue Forum in 2013. During his speech, he insisted on linking the two words 'terrorism' and 'Islam', and refused to take back his comments after one of the attendees expressed an objection. This was surprising because Mr Hague, in particular, is among the most eloquent and diplomatic British politicians I have seen in recent years. But then again, the general mood had changed between 2005 and 2013, and Mr. Hague would have only been echoing his party line.

---

6 Source: *ABC Chicago*, August 2016: https://abc7chicago.com/mccain-defends-obama-arab-2008-campaign-john/4058948/

7 Source: *Hansard*, September 2005: https://publications.parliament.uk/pa/cm200506/cmselect/cmhaff/uc462-i/uc46202.htm

Things obviously went further south for the UK during the campaign for, and after, the 2016 Brexit vote. Of course, Brexiteers will tell you that the UK, despite its current economic pains, will eventually be better off. They will argue that what matters is that "we have made our decision," and that the country has taken back control. On the flip side, critics will cite the current state of the economy, newly imposed travel restrictions and inability to import much needed skilled labour.

Now, don't get me wrong — I have no dog in this fight, I respect that the people have spoken, and accept Brexit is now a reality that must be dealt with. Of course, exiting with a pre-existing plan would have been far better. However, what irked me the most was the accompanying campaign of fake news and xenophobia. This is rather alarming because, as what has happened in America, tolerating such rhetoric normalises nastiness, which is completely un-British! This creates a lot of concern and hostility. In 2017 I commissioned the British polling firm YouGov to run a poll for *Arab News* and it was established that 55% of Brits regard it as right to engage in state level racial profiling against Arabs and Muslims.[8]

I have seen vox pops of voters saying Brexit was a good decision because it would stop Muslims from coming into the UK (how this relates to leaving the EU, which is mostly Christian, I don't know). Not to mention the racism towards certain nationalities — such as the Polish — who were tainted for a long time as being here to "steal our jobs and take our benefits." To those saying such things, I respond with two points. Number one: good luck getting any plumbing done in your homes![9] And number two: Poland is likely to have a bigger economy than the UK by 2030, and has currently more growth than

---

8   https://caabu.org/news/news/press-release-55-brits-support-racial-profiling-against-arabs-and-muslims-arab-news-caabu-

9 "More than half of the 290,000 people who came into Britain after the expansion of the EU were from Poland." Source: *Financial Times*, February 2006: https://www.ft.com/content/8ba3470c-a38f-11da-83cc-0000779e2340

Britain — average annual UK growth over the last decade was 0.5% while in Poland it was 3.6%.[10]

Unsurprisingly, British media reports dating back to 2018 say hate crimes have doubled since the Brexit vote. Another thing I also now notice about London is the alarming increase in knife crime, theft and midday robberies.

Now, I know there is much criticism for former Prime Minister Boris Johnson, his premiership, and his handling of the pandemic; however, we have to be fair when it comes to his time as Mayor of London. I would definitely argue that he, and his predecessor Ken Livingstone, both did amazing jobs as Mayors of the British capital. Boris particularly added a lot of charm with his cycling and his love of stunts, such as attaching himself to a zipline to promote the 2012 Olympics.[11] Sadly, crime rates in London have soared to an astonishing high since current Mayor Sadiq Khan took office: over 912,000 police-recorded crimes in 2019/20 compared to 744,000 in 2015/16.[12]

Of course, with three different prime ministers in the last five years, the revolving door at Number 10 has also stripped the UK of one of its most important perceptions: political stability. Naturally, both Brexit and the pandemic played a vital role in the short life spans of several leaders; infamously, Liz Truss and her 'trickle-down' economic theory couldn't outlive a lettuce head.[13] (She was, incidentally, the last PM to serve under the late Queen Elizabeth.)

But life is all about ups and downs. This is as true for individuals as

---

10 Source: *New European*, May 2023: https://www.theneweuropean.co.uk/when-poland-overtakes-the-uk/#:~:text=The%20inevitable%20progress%20of%20growth,than%20the%20UK%20by%202030.

11 Source: *The Guardian*, August 2012: https://www.theguardian.com/politics/2012/aug/01/boris-johnson-zip-wire

12 Source: Statista, March 2024: https://www.statista.com/topics/4627/crime-in-london/#editorsPicks

13 Source: *Newsweek*, October 2022: https://www.newsweek.com/liz-truss-resign-uk-prime-minister-cabbage-daily-star-mockery-latest-update-1753522

it is for nations. British history is full of great leaders who managed to turn the country's fortunes around, and revive both its economy and image. Whoever comes next to No 10 Downing Street needs to resist the need for appeasement, reject populism and secure buy-in for a long-term plan for Britain, which the country desperately needs.

For his part, King Charles III is seen — at least from afar — as a unifying figure in the country. I was very saddened to hear of his cancer and I speak for many in our part of the world when I saw we do wish him well and hope for a speedy recovery. As I mentioned in the Absent in the Spring chapter, I met him in 2008, when he was still the Prince of Wales, and was taken by his humility and sincere care for the environment and the planet. Naturally, King Charles enjoys a lot of respect in the Gulf region, where deep personal ties link His Majesty to members of Arab royal families. As I mentioned in that chapter, the then Prince hosted a joint art gallery in my country with Prince Khaled Al Faisal, son of the late King Faisal bin Abdulaziz. Very few statesmen around the world enjoy such close, and enduring, relationships.

Of course, I am aware that there are republicans in the UK, and again, they are free to be as anti-monarchy as they would like. However, as an Anglophile, I would say in times of crises, nations need unity, and need to build on their assets. I would not be the first to argue that the Royal Family is a major asset for this country as long as its members behave responsibly. It is also probably the strongest, and one of the few remaining, British brands.

"Without them, the country would be a lot less interesting", renowned Nation Brand expert Simon Anholt told my newspaper, *Arab News*, recently. He evaluates the net value of what the Royal Family brings into the British economy to be in billions: "They cost taxpayers several millions a year, sometimes many millions a year, to keep them there. But what they actually return to the country's image in terms of pure brand value is in the order of billions. People love monarchies, especially people who don't live in monarchies themselves."[14]

And continuing with the need to build on assets, I think the British Government would be well advised to forge stronger ties with Gulf Countries. A free-trade agreement would be the UK's best bet following Brexit, as European trade policy expert Paul McGrade has argued recently in my own newspaper, *Arab News*. As he points out, there is little likelihood in the short term of a free-trade agreement for the UK with either America or India, since the former is now tied up with internal domestic politics and the latter is currently absorbed with issues around protectionism. He goes as far as saying that the Gulf Co-operation Council of Bahrain, Kuwait, Oman, Qatar, Saudi Arabia and the United Arab Emirates are fast becoming a modern-day Venice in terms of global trade.[15] This is especially true of Saudi Arabia. The two countries have a lot to exchange in terms of expertise and skilled workforce. While the emerging and evolving Saudi needs in mining, energy, defense, education and transportation are all great opportunities for cooperation.

A final word would be that while a lot can change in twenty years, one has also to remember that 2004 was also not that long ago. In other words, the United Kingdom can still make a come-back, rediscover for itself a new place on the global scene and thrive once again.

At this moment in time, what both Kingdoms need to remember, in my opinion, is, to quote the wise words often attributed to Winston Churchill:[16]

"Success is not final, failure is not fatal;
it is the courage to continue that counts."

---

14 Source: *Arab News*, November 2022: https://www.arabnews.com/node/2207111/middle-east

15 Source: *Arab News*, January 2023: https://www.arabnews.com/tags/paul-mcgrade

16 Many wise quotations circulating on the internet are frequently mistakenly attributed to the late Winston Churchill but historians question whether there is any satisfactory evidence to confirm that this particular saying was actually one of his.